LIFT UP
YOUR HEAD,
TOM DOOLEY

The True Story
of the Appalachian Murder
That Inspired
One of America's
Most Popular Ballads

John Foster West

ISBN No. 1-878086-20-0

Library of Congress Catalog Card Number 93-071246

Printed in the United States of America

Book design: Elizabeth House
Illustrations: Joel Trussel
Art Assistance: Bill Bailey

Down Home Press
P.O. Box 4126
Asheboro, N.C. 27204

Other books by John Foster West:

up ego!

Time Was

The Ballad of Tom Dula

Appalachian Dawn

This Proud Land

Wry Wine

The Summer People

FOREWORD

Caldwell County, North Carolina
Friday, May 25, 1866

The fields were still dark, the stars still shining when Laura Foster was awakened by a man's voice, low but urgent, at the window. Her sleep had been shallow and troubled; quickly she was up and out of her father's farmhouse, moving silent as a shadow.

Tom Dula met her in the dewy mountain darkness. They stood close, talking softly.

It was no secret that Tom and Laura were lovers; Wilson Foster, Laura's father, told people that his daughter shared her bed with Tom, not only under her father's roof but right before his rather casual eyes, as well.

But on this morning, stealth was expedient. Laura did not want to wake the household. She did not want to arouse her father's curiosity.

For two things were about to happen: she was about to leave the place and her four younger, motherless siblings in the sole care of her father, and – more certain to invoke the old man's anger – she was leaving on his horse.

Whatever was said between Tom and Laura on that morning, the conference was brief. Tom soon left, on foot. Laura hurried back into the house and put on two dresses, one made of store-bought goods and one of checked homespun, which she pinned at the bosom with a small ornamental brooch. She caught up her chestnut hair with a fine-toothed comb, flung her cape over her shoulders, bundled a change of clothes and made a swift and silent exit.

There was no time to saddle her father's mare; the sky was growing pale in the east and birds were waking. Laura untied the homemade tether from the hitching tree, swung an agile leg over the horse's bare back, settled her belongings in her lap, and set out on a fateful journey.

Following a road along the Yadkin River, she rode downstream, toward the sunrise. Did she expect to overtake Tom Dula? If so, she was disappointed. When he left her father's he took a different path, rougher, shorter by a mile to their mutual destination.

Even walking, Tom would likely get there first for he had been cradled and schooled by nature in the country they would pass through. His widowed mother owned several thousand acres of those coves and mountainsides; the Dulas were materially a notch or so above most of their neighbors, though the war-deaths of Tom's two Confederate-soldier brothers left the land with no man much inclined to work it.

Draft animals, used up by the war, were scarce. Cash was scarce. Thus Tom had no horse to ride. But he was young and strong, a dark-haired, good-looking, fiddling ex-drummer boy with the rigors of the war just a year behind him. And his feet took him easily in all sorts of directions.

Within a mile Laura did meet someone on the road, a community washerwoman named Betsy Scott. "Have you seen Tom this morning?" Mrs. Scott asked.

"He came by the house before day," said Laura. Then she confided, "He said to meet him at the Bates Place. We're fixing to get married."

Tom Dula's facility with the hearts (and more) of women had been a legend along the Yadkin from his early teens. Betsy Scott was probably aware that he was entertaining other women with the same open intimacy that for the past two months he had enjoyed with Laura. She may also have sensed an anxiety that Laura left unspoken: very possibly, Laura Foster was pregnant.

Aware also of how short-lived a promise of marriage from Tom Dula might be, Mrs. Scott pressed her neighbor to move on. "I would have been further on the road by this time," she cautioned.

The Bates Place lay six miles east of Wilson Foster's, in Wilkes County. Once the site of a busy blacksmith shop, it was long abandoned and even the shop-site had grown up in brushy woods and laurel thickets.

Laura's journey there would not be swift. Her father had started to re-shoe the horse, half-trimmed its hooves and got distracted before the new shoes were made. Its gait was awkward, maybe even pained, as it picked its way along the road. One hoof left a peculiar, pointed track.

The rider did not feel too well herself. Her shoulders were broken out in tender welts she thought were part of The Disease. She had syphilis; called it by its common name: The Pock. Small matter now; Tom had it too.

And anyway, it didn't show. Gossips would not see it. From their reports she was a pretty woman, though she had a gap between her front teeth. She was older than Tom by less than a year; he would be 22, himself, the 20th of June. Some over-watchful people said of her, "She has round heels." That meant she spent more time in her bed than on her feet. The more polite said she was "beautiful – but frail."

"Frail" in that text had nothing to do with fragile health. It had to do with moral stamina. Over in Wilkes County, near where she was headed, Laura had two female cousins who were designated "frail," as well, though vigorous and boisterous in certain other ways. Later on this very morning Tom would visit them.

Probably not even Tom and Ann Foster Melton, themselves, could remember when they began to sleep together. Conveniently, they had grown up neighbors, perhaps a half a mile apart. The first time Ann's mother paid enough attention to their activity to take offense, Ann and Tom were in their mid-teens and Ann was already married to James Melton. Ann's mother, Lotty Foster, may have had some respect for the bonds of marriage though she herself had borne all five of her children without becoming legally encumbered. At any rate, she made note that she had once indignantly chased Tom naked from Ann's bed.

For his part, James Melton, by all accounts a good and decent man, seemed to pay no mind at all to what Ann did with Tom. He ran a farm and was the local cobbler; he kept busy. There were three beds in his one-room cabin and he slept alone in one of them; that Tom and Ann frequently shared another appeared of little consequence. Ann was a mesmerizingly beautiful creature; that may have been enough for him. Also, Ann was imperious, aggressive and ferocious when thwarted. That may have contributed to her husband's passiveness, as well.

Another dimension had come in March to this menage with the arrival of Ann's and Laura's cousin Pauline Foster. On the pretense of visiting her grandfather, Pauline came to Wilkes County from neighboring Watauga to see the only doctor in that whole mountain region. Probably not aware of the true nature of her affliction, James and Ann Melton took her in. They agreed to pay her to help with the house and farm work, probably a great relief to James, for Ann disdained chores of any sort.

Pauline Foster may have been, in fact, the first of these dramatis personae to be absolutely known to have The Pock. Early after her arrival, she visited the barn and the woods with Tom Dula – among others. By summer, she would declare (not shyly) to a neighbor, "We ALL have it."

"All," through whatever route, included Tom Dula, Laura Foster, Ann and James Melton.

Yet curiously, maybe because Pauline had sought treatment, Ann and Tom both pointed to another source: Laura Foster. Tom told the doctor Laura had infected him. Ann, subjected to the prescription of the time – remedies which ring yet with dreadful overtones: blue stone, blue mass, caustic – was furious.

Ann was also jealous. Not of Pauline, who was no better than she had to be, in looks, word or deed. Despite occasional shared adventures, Pauline was no serious contender for the affections of Tom Dula.

Ann was jealous of Laura Foster.

One morning on his way home from church, Tom talked bitterly with an elder friend about his newfound illness. "I am going to put through the one that gave it to me," he declared.

"Tom, I wouldn't do that," the old man answered.

Had Laura Foster known of the events of the night before her supposed wedding day, as she rode into that May morning, she might have turned the horse around and gone back to face her father's brief and unimpressive wrath.

On Thursday, Tom had walked from his mother's place to Lotty Foster's and borrowed a mattock. He told Ann's brother Tom he "wanted to work out some devilment." Seen later digging on the road farther along the ridge, he told a passing neighbor that he was widening the road so that he could more easily walk at night.

Ann secured that day a quart canteen of bootleg whiskey. About three that Thursday afternoon, Tom and Ann disappeared. They were gone all night.

What Laura observed as she approached the Bates Place will never be known. Whether Tom was there to meet her, or whether she tethered the horse to a dogwood tree and went to look for him, or – exactly – what transpired when she arrived, and who all was involved – will not be known.

Pauline Foster told that Ann came in on Friday morning, took off her wet dress and shoes, and crawled into bed beside her. Later, after Pauline had gotten up to do the chores, Tom came and stood over the bed and held a whispered conference with Ann.

Wilson Foster came to Melton's a little later, on that Friday. Ann was still in bed; James and Pauline were working elsewhere. If Ann knew where Laura Foster had gone – with Wilson Foster's horse – she yawned and would not say. Discouraged, Laura's father left.

Tom spent part of the day home at his mother's, in bed. Sometime late in the day he went out for a while to work around the barn, his mother said. That night he moaned in his sleep, as though in a fever.

Sometime on that Friday, Tom met Laura in the woods. In one quick, forceful motion, he plunged into her chest cavity the long blade of a knife. Then, perhaps with the help of Ann, he transported the body about half a mile to the grave he had dug with the mattock on the night before. Into that hole, about two and a half feet deep, he dumped the body on its right side, with its legs drawn up.

The marriage bed Tom Dula had prepared for his bride-to-be was not even large enough for one.

That Tom was at home, in the coming days, and Laura nowhere in sight was fast becoming a puzzle, up and down the hollows. News traveled; Laura had told Betsy Scott that she and Tom were going to get married.

In one sense, Wilson Foster's mind was put at ease the next day. On Saturday, his mare came home, the chewed tether dragging. It took a few days for the community to begin to truly worry about the disappearance of a young woman of shaded reputation. It took little time at all for Tom Dula's involvement to be the meat at every table. For one thing, Tom had spoken cavalierly, when someone asked about the rumored wedding. "I have no use for Laura Foster," he had said. And then, he took no part in the ensuing searches.

At last, when a month went by without a sign of Laura, Tom came to Ann downcast and told her that suspicion against him was so strong that he would have to go away. The two lay in her bed and wept. They clung to each other weeping, as he got ready to depart.

He would find a haven, he said to Pauline, and come back for Ann and his mother. He left, then, and went to Tennessee.

Once out of Wilkes Tom changed his name to Hall. Just across the state line from Watauga County he got a job on the James Grayson farm, at Trade, Tennessee. In late June, when he had worked there just long enough to buy some boots to replace those he had worn out in his flight, two deputies came from Wilkes County.

This time Tom Dula did not have to walk. James Grayson, a Tennessee legislator, transported the bound prisoner behind him on his horse as they returned Tom to the Wilkes County Jail, on a charge of murder. As yet there was no corpse.

But there were clues. Late in June, searchers found the severed horse-tether tied to a dogwood tree at the Bates Place. Nearby they found another place where the horse apparently had stood for a while – at least long enough to do its business twice. And near that place there was a darkened, stinking spot of earth. Someone had bled to death there, investigators figured. Someone had been murdered on that spot.

The Law did not take wholly seriously Pauline Foster's jocular claim before two deputies: "Me and Tom Dula killed Laura Foster." She was held temporarily, deemed, perhaps, too silly to be guilty, and turned loose. The more accepted idea was that Ann Melton and Tom Dula killed Laura Foster, at a place and by a means yet to be discovered.

It was true that Pauline knew where the body was buried. Worried that rains or animals might have uncovered the corpse, and apparently afraid to go tend to it by herself, Ann coerced Pauline into going with her up what is now called Laura Foster Ridge. Pauline was so terrified that she risked Ann's full-blown abuse and refused to go the whole distance. But Ann showed her where the body lay.

Shortly, Ann was arrested and put into a jail cell next to Tom's. More in fear now of being prosecuted, herself, than she needed to fear an incarcerated Ann, Pauline became the principal witness in a case that would proceed – and conclude – largely on her testimony.

On the first day of September, a search party paused to rest as the men were making their way along the ridge near the Bates Place. A horse standing near a laurel thicket began to whinny. Aware that it might have smelled something the men could not, the searchers cut poles and began testing the ground. One of the poles found a soft place. The grave.

The body of Laura Foster lay with her trousseau, of sorts, covering her upturned face.

On October 1, 1866, the Grand Jury of Wilkes County was summoned to hear evidence in the murder. A true bill was returned, indicting Tom Dula for murder and Ann Melton for "maliciously, feloniously, violently, and in her malice aforethought" inciting and abetting Dula in the crime. Both entered a plea of Not Guilty.

For reasons known only to himself, the state's most illustrious lawyer, former North Carolina governor Zebulon Vance, took on the defense of the state's most notorious scoundrel – who had no money to pay him.

Vance tried valiantly; he was able to accomplish two things for Tom Dula. First, he got the trial moved away from the passions of Wilkes County, down to the Iredell County seat of Statesville. That done, he next got Dula's case separated from Ann Melton's.

Nonetheless, on Sunday morning, Oct. 21, 1866, a Superior Court jury returned a verdict of guilty, and Tom Dula was sentenced to hang.

An appeal gained a new trial, which came to the same conclusion. Ann Melton remained in jail for most of the two years between the murder and the case's end. But she was never called to testify, and Tom Dula would neither name her as his accomplice nor exonerate her.

At last, on April 30, 1868, Tom sent for a lawyer, to whom he handed a penciled note. "Statement of Thomas C. Dula – I declare that I am the only person that had any hand in the murder of Laura Foster." Ann Melton would, after a weary and perfunctory semblance of a trial, go free.

On May 1, 1868, a cart bearing Tom Dula, sitting on his coffin, flanked by his devoted sister Eliza and her husband made its way through a throng unequalled, to that day, on the street at Statesville, North Carolina. It paused under the gallows, where Dula was allowed to speak, his neck already in the noose, for close to an hour about the wages of sin and the tragedy of his betrayal by neighbors whom he said bore false witness against him.

Then, the relatives were removed, the cart jerked from beneath him, and Tom Dula left to hang until he was dead.

Tom Dula died, in the words of a New York Herald reporter on the scene, "a wretch who well knew he was going into eternity with an unconfessed murder upon his mind and falsehood upon his lips."

And that is the whole truth.

Or else it is not.

Read on.

ACKNOWLEDGEMENTS

I wish to express my warmest thanks to Mrs. Charlotte Barnes of Matthews for her information dealing with Tom Dula's lineage and the location of Ann Melton's grave. Mrs. Barnes and her husband, Bill, have done a movie documentary on the Tom Dula-Laura Foster murder case.

I am also greatly indebted to Mr. John Bramell (TVA/ARC) of Knoxville, Tennessee, for his cooperation in our visits to Wilkes County and to Statesville to obtain information on the Dula-Foster murder case and for supplying photographs and maps used in this book.

I appreciated the assistance given me by the personnel of the Iredell County Library, especially that of Ms. Margie Wessells and Mr. David Bunch, a volunteer in the James Iredell House.

Finally, I would like to express my appreciation to Ms. Joan Baity, director of Old Wilkes Inc., the museum located in the old Wilkes County Jail, where Tom Dula and Ann Melton were incarcerated, for her attention to my needs in gathering details for *Lift Up Your Head, Tom Dooley.*

CONTENTS

INTRODUCTION

Lift Up Your Head, Tom Dooley is the second book I have written about the Tom Dula-Laura Foster murder case. The first, *The Ballad of Tom Dula*, was published in 1970 and went through several printings during the decade it remained available, before the publisher declared bankruptcy and returned the remnants to me.

I continue to receive letters from folklore buffs wanting to obtain a copy of the book or to discuss the story with me. Old Wilkes, Inc., a gift shop and museum in Wilkesboro, where Tom Dula and Ann Melton were incarcerated, has continued to sell the book over the years without advertising, to visitors from many parts of the world.

One might wonder why I am writing a second book on the subject. The answer is simple: *The Ballad of Tom Dula* was mainly technical, built around the old mountain ballad that evolved from the case. It emphasized legal documents and historical references and used a scholarly presentation, making it necessary for readers to dig through complicated details to understand the story. This book is an attempt to tell the true story behind the old ballad in chronological order, in a language clear and precise. Citing documents within the narration will be limited and will not intrude into the continuity.

Following the section dealing with the story of the Tom Dula-Laura Foster murder case and its consequences, the end of the book contains a supplementary section of legal documents, contemporary newspaper articles, source titles, etc.

A point needs to be made concerning names. Dula was pronounced

Dooley in the old ballad. Mountain people have always pronounced the name Dooley, as we did in the schools I attended as a child with Dula children. Furthermore, semi-literate census takers in the mid-nineteenth century spelled it Dooley, Duly, Doolie, etc. And the name Laura has always been pronounced Laurie in the hills of North Carolina.

After the lapse of more than a century, discovering the truth behind the old ballad is possible only by studying legal documents relating to the case and by reading contemporary newspaper articles. The "Tom Dooley" ballad and its variants give little information. Folk tales about Tom Dula told over the decades have been woefully inaccurate.

Recently, a town official told a crew doing a television documentary in Wilkesboro that Tom Dula was hanged from the town's renowned old Tory Oak, more than 22 years after my first book detailed Dula's two trials and execution from a gallows in Statesville. Another citizen was heard to say that he was related to James Grayson, the sheriff of Wilkes County at the time of Tom's arrest; whereas legal documents clearly record the fact that the sheriff of Wilkes was William Hix and that James Grayson was a citizen of Tennessee. I want to dispose of such modern misconceptions once again for anyone interested in learning the truth instead of believing old folk tales.

In addition, a new generation of readers deserves to know the facts behind the "Tom Dooley" ballad, which refuse to fade into oblivion.

Concerning directions used in the book: Although the Yadkin River runs northeast through Happy Valley and Elkville, in writing about the area I have found it simpler to indicate that the river flows from south to north and that the left side is to the west, and the right to the east.

Anyone wishing to visit Elkville today can do so by driving 11.2 miles north from U.S. 321, starting five miles west of Lenoir; by traveling Highway 268, 18 miles south from U.S. 421 at Wilkesboro to Elk Creek; or by turning left from U.S. 421 onto Mt. Pleasant Road, 11 miles west of Wilkesboro and driving south-southeast to Highway 268 at Ferguson. A fourth way is possible by turning right from U.S. 421 onto State Road 1508 five miles northeast of Boone, passing through the community of Triplett, and following the Elk Creek Road; but much of it is unpaved and rocky, with sharp, blind curves.

As a visitor travels north on Highway 268, he will not find that the old Stony Fork Road branches off to the left as soon as he crosses Elk Creek, as indicated in a crudely drawn map used as evidence in Tom Dula's trials. Today, it is necessary to turn left and follow the Elk

Creek Road (State Road 1159) 1.6 miles west, before turning right onto the Stony Fork Road, recently re-named the Gladys Fork Road by the State Department of Transportation. The old Stony Fork Road (Gladys Fork) crosses Reedy Branch, one mile from the Elk Creek Road, Laura Foster Ridge, and a good many hills and hollows, before ending 3.6 miles north of Elk Creek at State Road 1135, which connects with the Mt. Pleasant Road some distance to the northeast and leads to Highway 268 at Ferguson.

John Foster West
Emeritus Professor of English
Appalachian State University

THE
PLACE

Beginning as a spring near the continental divide at Green Park Inn in Blowing Rock, North Carolina, the Yadkin River flows in a south-southeasterly direction, down through the mountains and hills until it reaches Patterson, in Caldwell County, some 15 miles from its source. There, it takes an almost 90-degree turn to the left and flows northeast into Wilkes County, past the communities of Elkville and Ferguson and the towns of Wilkesboro, North Wilkesboro, and Elkin. Near Elkin, the river turns southeastward. Swollen by tributaries, it later becomes one of the Southeast's major rivers, the Pee Dee, as it moves toward South Carolina and the Atlantic Ocean.

The region between Patterson and Ferguson has been called Happy Valley since early days. Over a century ago the county line between Caldwell and Wilkes Counties passed through the community of Elk Creek. It was there, in the area along the Yadkin River, that Laura Foster was murdered in May, 1866.

Professor Elisha Mitchell (for whom Mount Mitchell is named) jotted down in his notes while on a geological exploration of the valley in the summer of 1828: "This upper valley to the Yadkin is delightful;

from half a mile wide, bounded by ranges of mountains of moderate size, the Brushy Mountains on one side and a small chain parallel to the Blue Ridge on the other; the land is very fertile, pleasant to cultivate and produces immense quantities of corn; the air is salubrious and healthy and the soil occupied by very respectable farms."

Although there were earlier settlers on smaller farms, such as Daniel Boone and my own grandfather four generations removed, Alexander West I, large plantations began to spring up along the Yadkin River in Happy Valley as early as the 1780's. Along the river north of Elk Creek, Benjamin Howard settled soon after marrying in Baltimore in 1772, and was there when Daniel Boone lived on Beaver Creek, before he left for Kentucky in 1774. (One of the earliest houses, the old Harris home, is still standing and occupied today, just across NC 268 from Eller's Store and 150 yards north of Elk Creek.)

At the end of the Revolutionary War, Captain William Dula, a pioneering former soldier from Virginia, came into the valley. He obtained many acres of land up and down the river and located his six children on large prosperous plantations in Happy Valley. Two sons and four daughters were deeded land reaching from below Elkville all the way upstream to Patterson, 13 miles to the south. The sons were William Beesly and Thomas B. Dula; the daughters – Nancy, Mildred, Sarah, and Elizabeth – married, respectively, Cuthbert Jones, William Horton, David Eagles Horton, and John Witherspoon (for whom my grandfather, John Witherspoon West, was named).

In addition to their six children, there issued from Captain Dula and his wife 50 grandchildren and 150 great grandchildren, according to a book written about the valley, *World of My Childhood*, by the Rev. Robert L. Isbell. Many of them became doctors, lawyers, and successful businessmen. These plantation owners and a few others were the aristocrats, the elite of Happy Valley. They associated only with each other and intermarried, many couples being double first cousins.

Other families, less fortunate, settled the upland bordering the rich Yadkin River bottomland. They either owned their own small patches of land or tended the hillside fringes of the plantations. They were not used as tenants in the river bottom lands before the Civil War because of slavery. After the War, many of these poor farmers became sharecroppers on the former plantations, continuing to live in their one- or two-room pole cabins among the hills.

As one generation followed another, hardships for the upland farmers increased until they became poverty-stricken and demoralized during and following the Civil War, while the land-rich plantation owners, although no longer prosperous with slave labor, at least continued to hold their own. One of the earlier, more fortunate land owners among the upland farmers, according to Charlotte Barnes of Matthews, North Carolina, who researched the Dula family for a television documentary, was Capt. William Dula's brother, grandfather of Tom Dula. Part of his land lay along Reedy Branch, where Tom Dula's widowed mother, Mary, lived in 1866 and where Tom was born.

As has been implied, the aristocrats of Happy Valley had little to do with the "pore white trash" living in the surrounding hills and absolutely nothing to do with them socially. The Rev. Isbell writes in his book that there were good people among the hill folk, but he seems to admit this with condescension.

Among the poor people who became tenant farmers at the end of slavery were Wilson Foster, Laura Foster's father, and later her brother James. Both worked land belonging to the Rev. Isbell's uncle.

Of the landlord-tenant relationship the Rev. Isbell wrote: "It was an unheard of thing to invite the tenant class to take part in the socials of the land owners; however pretty the girls might be or handsome the men, custom barred their mingling together in social life." This same custom separated the classes at the time of Laura Foster's murder.

The Fosters, upland Dulas, Meltons, Scotts, Halls – almost all those involved in the two trials of Tom Dula – were from among the class living in the uplands, with the exception of a few witnesses who were landowners, such as Col. James Isbell and Dr. George Carter.

From the article on Tom Dula's execution in the New York *Herald* comes this excerpt:

> *The community in the vicinity of this tragedy is divided into two entirely separate and distinct classes. The one occupying the fertile lands adjacent to the Yadkin River and its tributaries, is educated and intelligent, and the other, living on the spurs and ridges of the mountains, is ignorant, poor, and depraved. A state of immorality unexampled in the history of any country exists among these people, and with such a system of freeloveism prevails that it is "a wise child that knows its father." ... It is a poor country, covered with thickets and dense undergrowth.*

Although a wide social gap between the hill folk and the river dwellers did exist, the Yankee reporter exaggerated the social conditions among the hill folk. The Wests have lived among these people since 1772, and I was born among them. Although depraved families did exist, living on adjacent hillsides or beyond the next ridge could be found the most industrious, honest, and moral families living in any society.

Calvin J. Cowles moved from Hamptonville in 1846 and established a store at the mouth of Elk Creek, according to *World of My Childhood*. Elkville Post Office was also established at Cowles Store, which remained the name of the establishment after Calvin Cowles moved to Wilkesboro in 1858.

The store and post office were the heart of the Elkville community. The Rev. Isbell writes that the store was the gathering place for all of Elk Creek and Stony Fork communities and for those living up and down the Yadkin River for miles in both directions. Almost everything that came through that part of the county in the way of shows and entertainment played at Elkville, the Rev. Isbell continues. It was a noted place and muster ground for the militia. During political campaigns great crowds came to hear candidates speak. A Justice of the Peace held court at Cowles Store, and deputy sheriffs were dispatched from this rural "courthouse," as were Jack Adkins and Ben Ferguson, who were sent into Tennessee after Tom Dula.

Today, Eller's Store, a combination service station-grocery store, is the local gathering place, near where Cowles Store once stood, but the post office has moved two miles down-river to Ferguson. If you are not in a hurry and it is a rainy day, local men of all ages will be at the store to talk to you about the history and folklore of Happy Valley.

TROUBLED TIMES

To understand how much Tom Dula was a victim of civil and political conditions of his time, one needs to know something about those conditions. President Lincoln had begun reconstruction of the South well before the end of the Civil War in areas occupied by Union Forces. In December, 1863, he proclaimed that if 10 percent of the 1860 voting population of a state took the necessary Oath of Allegiance – first established in Louisiana, Tennessee, Virginia, and Arkansas – that state could take its place in the new nation which had replaced the former Union.

Lincoln's lenient plan initiated bitter conflict between the President and the radical wing of the Republican Party in Congress. The radicals' more restrictive plan was reflected in the Wade-Davis Bill of July, 1864. While Congress was not in session, Lincoln killed the bill with a pocket veto. Later, the assassination of President Lincoln in April, 1865, brought Vice-President Andrew Johnson into the presidency.

Essentially, the Civil War ended at Appomattox Courthouse on April 9, 1865. On April 29, General John Schofield, federal officer in charge of North Carolina, issued a proclamation declaring hostilities over and divided the state into three districts, with Gen. Jacob D. Cox having jurisdiction over Western North Carolina.

On the same day, President Johnson issued his Amnesty Proclamation, which pardoned all who would swear allegiance to the United States and to the Constitution, excepting all high civil and military officials of the Confederacy, all who had required slaves to join the Confederacy, and all persons with assets of more than $20,000. Even those excepted could request pardon.

President Johnson's Amnesty Proclamation alienated the Republican radicals in Congress. On the first day of the new session in December, 1865, Congress refused to seat the members recently elected in Southern states and created its own Joint Committee of Reconstruction. In the election of 1866, Johnson's angry opposition, the refusal of the Southern states to accept the 14th Amendment, race riots, etc., allowed the Republican radicals a complete victory.

The same day President Johnson issued his Amnesty Proclamation, he appointed William W. Holden provisional governor of North Carolina. Holden, publisher and editor of the North Carolina *Standard*, a newspaper located in Raleigh, had opposed continuation of the war well before its end and had run unsuccessfully against Governor Vance in the election of 1864, as a member of the Peace Party. His paper was suspended the same year. Holden was replaced as governor the same year when Jonathan Worth was elected and inaugurated on December 28, 1865.

Congress's Reconstruction Acts of March, 1867, were passed to replace the forgiving plans of Lincoln and Johnson. The Southern states, other than Tennessee, were divided into five military districts, each commanded by a major general of the U.S. Army. Each general was to supervise the reconstruction of these states until a new state constitution could be approved by Congress. An attempt was made to impeach President Johnson, but failed by one vote. General Grant, wartime commander of the Union forces, was elected president in 1868. The last of the 10 embattled Southern states was not readmitted to the Union until July, 1870, well after Tom Dula's execution.

One other point ought to be made concerning conditions in the area Tom Dula returned to after the end of the Civil War. Many of those living in the western North Carolina mountains were not pro-South, and many were outright Unionists, a circumstance that divided families and caused conflicts between neighbors for the rest of the century. Tennessee was one of the first Confederate states to return to Union control before the war ended, and only Watauga County lay between Wilkes County and that state, a region wooded and mountainous.

As the war wound down, Confederate deserters from the mountains, who had wanted nothing to do with the war to start with, began to seek out the forests and hills of western Wilkes as a hiding place from Confederate soldiers sent to capture or shoot them. My father, who was born in 1867, used to tell me stories about deserters when I was a child, early in the twentieth century. In the Brushy Mountains, the brother of my great-grandfather (Foster) was hunted down and shot by the Home Guard because he refused to serve the Confederacy (although three of my great-uncles who were Wests served, and two were killed). I still own an ante-bellum muzzle-loading shotgun which was once owned by a deserter who was shot on the farm of my great-aunt, Nancy West, by a detail of Confederate soldiers.

Tom Dula returned from federal prison to this restless region, where not only society was in ferment, but where economic conditions even threatened starvation in many areas. Food was scarce, and what was available was raised locally. There was no such luxury as flour. Bread was made from coarsely hand-ground corn. Sweet potatoes and cowpeas were the staples. Instead of coffee or tea, the hillfolk were obliged to substitute sassafras tea, made from the ground dried bark of the sassafras shrub's roots, or "coffee" from crushed roasted acorns. Some pork was available to the few who could afford it. Honey and molasses were the only sweeteners to be had.

These economic conditions did not improve markedly for a decade after Tom Dula returned to Happy Valley.

THE
FATAL TRIANGLE

Tom Dula's mother, Mary, testified in court that he was 22 years old on June 20, 1866. That would have established his birth date as June 20, 1844 and his age at 21 on the date of Laura Foster's murder, May 25, 1866. Tom Dula's family was probably not as indigent as their immediate neighbors, an economic condition I had not assumed in my first book.

Charlotte Barnes traced the lineage of Thomas C. Dula by studying census records of the Elkville area and from other sources. She found that when Captain William B. Dula came into Happy Valley to settle in 1790, he was accompanied by a younger brother named Bennett Dula (I), who was born in 1760 and died in July, 1822. Whereas Captain Dula acquired thousands of acres of rich Yadkin River bottomland, Bennett Dula I settled on the upland west of the river in the vicinity of Reedy Branch. Bennett Dula I married Aney (possibly Amey) Stowe, and they had nine children.

Their second child was Thomas P. Dula, who married Mary Keaton in 1822. They were Tom Dula's parents. In the census of 1860, Mary Keaton Dula was listed as "head of household," which meant that her husband, Tom's father, had died sometime before that census was taken. These facts indicate that Tom Dula, listed as too poor to pay any of the cost of his two trials for murder and his appeal to the North Carolina Supreme Court, was the grand-nephew of Captain William Dula, the wealthiest land owner in Happy Valley, information I had not guessed in my first book and which folklore had never suggested.

Mary Dula owned the land the family lived on, along Reedy branch, land which was valued at $195 in 1860. Upland was valued at probably no more than five cents an acre at that time, a fact which would have indicated around 4,000 acres in Mary Dula's possession, but much of it probably consisted of rocky slopes or forests.

Besides Tom, there were three other children in Mary Dula's family. John, 10 years Tom's senior, was born in 1834 and Lenny A. (or Leny) was born in 1838, six years earlier than Tom. Mary Dula stated in her testimony that she had lost both of her older sons in the war, but whether they were killed or died of sickness was not revealed.

In addition to her three sons, Mary Dula had "a grown daughter," Eliza, living with her at the time of Tom Dula's first trial in October, 1866. Eliza, 20, was not listed among Mary's children in the census of 1860 and was probably already married to Anderson Dula, 37. Why she was living with her mother in 1866 cannot be known; however, her husband travelled to Statesville with her in late April, 1868, to claim Tom's corpse on May 1, after his execution.

Thomas C. Dula enlisted at Elkville in Wilkes County on March 15, 1862, as a private in Company K, 42nd Regiment, North Carolina Infantry, for three years or the duration of the war. The date indicates that Tom joined the army while still 17, three months before his 18th birthday. Various folk myths have been told or written about his war record. Some maintained that he joined the 26th Regiment (called infantry by some; by others, cavalry), for a while commanded by Col. Zebulon B. Vance – explaining why ex-Governor Vance came rushing to his defense during Tom's trials.

But Tom Dula's war record is available and indicates clearly his correct military unit. Other myths have Tom playing his banjo or fiddle for Col. Vance around campfires during bivouacs, and have him playing in the 26th Regiment's Johnny Reb band. Myths also maintained that Tom survived the war unscathed. All of these folk myths are untrue. His military record appears at the end of this book in the section on supplementary information.

The following description of Tom Dula appears in the Oath of Allegiance report which Tom signed with "his mark" when he was released as a prisoner of war from Point Lookout Prison in Maryland: hair – dark brown; eyes – brown; height – 5 ft. 9 1/2 in. The New York *Herald* reporter described Tom as being five feet, 11 inches tall, with dark eyes and dark, curly hair. The slight discrepancy between the two descriptions could be explained by the fact that the reporter viewed the prisoner from some distance away and that two years in the Statesville jail could have caused an emaciated Tom Dula to appear taller than he actually was. The reporter continued with Tom's description by writing, "though not handsome, he might be called good-looking."

As for Tom Dula's character, there can be no doubt that he was depraved, and the fact that he had served bravely during three years in a harsh war has little relevancy in the matter. His lechery did not come about as a result of the war, but had existed since childhood. Carlotta (Lotty) Foster, Ann Melton's mother, testified during the trials that she had caught Tom and Ann in bed together naked "two years before the war," when Ann was already the wife of James Melton. Since the war began in 1861, Tom would have been only 14 or 15 in 1859; Ann was about the same age. Lotty testified that Tom crawled under the bed when discovered, but she ordered him out.

How many women of the Happy Valley area Tom Dula had sexual relations with other than Ann Melton, Laura Foster, and Pauline Foster is a matter of conjecture. Once he and Ann quarreled over a woman named Caroline Barnes. There is some indication that he carried his lechery into the army with him. The *Herald* reporter wrote that some of his ex-military companions believed Tom had murdered the husband of a woman in Wilmington, North Carolina, during the war as the result of his "criminal intercourse" with her.

The *Herald* reporter wrote additionally that it was the opinion of these former companions who had come to Statesville to see Tom Dula executed, that he was "a terrible, desperate character and from their knowledge of his former career they had an anxious and singular curiosity to see how he would die."

The *Herald* reporter wrote further that "since the war closed, he has become reckless, demoralized, and a desperado, of whom the people in his vicinity had a terror." Yet there was a gentler side to Tom Dula's character, at least implied. Pauline Foster testified that when Tom was about to flee into Tennessee, he and Ann Melton embraced and wept, and Tom promised he would return Christmas for her and his mother. His final gesture of affection toward Ann was to write (or have written) a note on the last night of his life exonerating her from guilt in Laura Foster's murder.

How brave was Tom Dula? How determined? Oral tradition and all the facts indicate he was a brave soldier. The *Herald* reporter wrote that "he fought gallantly in the Confederate service, where he established a reputation for bravery." Washington Anderson testified: "I knew the general character of the prisoner while in the army. I was in the same company and regiment. His character was good as a soldier."

The fact that Tom fled into Tennessee is an indication of his willingness to resist the law. When he was captured by James Grayson, Jack Adkins, and Ben Ferguson, he apparently thought it was futile to resist, since Grayson carried a gun. However, the *Herald* reporter states that Tom tried to escape the next day on the way to the Wilkesboro jail. There is no record as to whether he tried to escape while in Wilkesboro, but the prosecutors at Statesville requested additional guards. At their insistence, the following court order was handed down:

> *It appears to the satisfaction of the Court that the insecurity of the jail of said county (Iredell) requires an additional guard for the safe keeping of the prisoner Thomas Dula in said prison. It is therefore ordered by the court that a guard of eight men be allowed the sheriff for the safe keeping of the prisoner Thomas Dula.*

Paying for eight guards would seem like an exorbitant cost for a county to accept unless the character and determination of the prisoner required it. And finally, as the noose became more imminent, Tom Dula apparently became more determined to escape. He was kept in leg chains. The *Herald* reporter wrote that the jailer, before he left Tom's cell the night before his execution, discovered his shackles were loose, a link of the chain having been filed through with a piece of window glass, which was found concealed in his bed. Anyone acquainted with cutting metal with a hacksaw can understand the long hours Tom Dula spent working on the link of a chain with a sliver of glass.

And Tom Dula died gamely. The *Herald* reporter wrote: "The fall was about two feet, and the neck was not broken. He did not struggle." Ten minutes passed before his heart ceased to beat; he was throttled instead of dying with a broken neck.

There is very little on record concerning a description of Laura Foster. Folklore describes her as beautiful, with chestnut hair, blue (or green or brown) eyes, and a friendly disposition. The *Herald* reporter wrote that she was "beautiful but frail." Pauline Foster, the State's witness, testified that her teeth were large and that there was a large open space between her teeth, not a missing tooth but a "natural space right in the center of her mouth."

Laura Foster was a poor girl, 21 years of age at the time of her death. She was the daughter of Wilson Foster, 63 years old in 1866, and of a mother who was 48 at the time of the 1860 census but who had died before Laura's murder. At the time of the census Laura Foster had three brothers and one sister, all younger than she: James, 11; Elbert, eight; John, six; and Elizabeth, an infant. Wilson Foster was a tenant farmer who lived at German Hill (earlier called Cilly), west of the Yadkin River and five miles south of Elkville, in Caldwell County.

Evidence presented during Tom Dula's trials proves without doubt that Laura Foster had "round heels," a mountain folk term for being promiscuous. But there was no hint of such a fault spoken by the people of Happy Valley during the century or more following the murder. "I never heerd no fault agin the gal," was the way one local man stated his opinion of Laura's character.

Many of the people who lived in the area were surprised when my first book was published to hear that the State's motive for the murder was that Laura Foster had communicated syphilis to Tom Dula, who passed it on to Ann Melton, leading to a "revenge" murder. Some of the readers condemned me and my book for conveying such outrageous charges against this good and decent girl, who was so cruelly murdered. Folk belief had always contended that the motive for the murder resulted from the fact that Ann Melton was jealous of Tom and Laura.

Ann Melton was a unique character, possessing almost all the faults one woman could have. She was probably born in 1843, and was 23 at the time of Laura Foster's murder. According to the *Herald* reporter, she was "the illegitimate daughter of Carlotta (Lotty) Foster," who lived in a cabin on a ridge, just above the Stony Fork Road and above Reedy Branch to the north. Besides Ann, Lotty Foster had one other daughter and three sons in 1866, all of them illegitimate: Thomas, age unknown; Martha, 11; Lenny, eight; and Marshall, three. The entire family was illiterate. In addition to her promiscuity, Lotty Foster had a reputation for drunkenness. This was the home Ann Foster Melton, the oldest of five children, had been born into and had grown up in until she was married at 14 or 15 to James Melton in 1858 or '59. The *Herald* reporter, in 1868, at Tom Dula's execution, wrote, "She is apparently twenty-five years of age, is the illegitimate daughter of one Carlotta Foster, and is a most beautiful woman. She is entirely uneducated, and though living in the midst of depravity and ignorance, has the manner and bearing of an accomplished lady, and all the natural poise that would grace a born beauty." That was the impression that Ann made on a reporter after having been incarcerated in a primitive jail cell for two years.

Although it is true that Ann Melton had grown up "in the midst of depravity," she seems to have adapted well to such an environment. The fact that she was already married in her mid-teens and was having sexual relations with Tom Dula after her marriage to another man indicates a lot about her character. One wonders just how young she was when she became sexually active. With a mother like Lotty Foster, she could have been quite young. According to records she seems to have had sexual relations with only her husband and Tom Dula, but Col. Isbell stated during the trials that "it was generally reported Ann Melton indulged in illicit intercourse with others besides the prisoner." Pauline Foster's testimony seems to indicate that Ann cohabited with Tom to the exclusion of even her husband.

In addition to her promiscuity, Ann Melton was temperamental, demanding, and aggressive. She was also lazy, with no interest in household duties.

THE
MURDER

Tom Dula's relationship with Ann Melton, which had started as early as three years before he joined the Confederate Army, probably resumed soon after he returned to his Reedy Branch home from a federal prison in the early summer of 1865. He lived in a convenient location for such a liaison, only about a half-mile from Lotty Foster's cabin on the ridge above Reedy Branch, just west of the Stony Fork Road. James Melton and Ann lived only a short distance beyond Lotty Foster, further west. Had it been necessary, Tom and Ann could have met in the woods surrounding the narrow valley through which Reedy Branch flowed. But, according to Pauline Foster's testimony, they did not have to yield to such inconvenience. Instead, they used one of three beds in James Melton's house while he slept in another.

The testimony of Wilson Foster, Laura's father, indicates that Tom reestablished his relationship with Laura early in 1866. The father stated that he had seen the two of them in bed together "once or twice." How Tom had come to know Laura is not recorded. She lived five miles upriver, in Caldwell County, but in a rural area with a scattered population, five miles is hardly a distance that will hinder neighbors

14

from knowing one another, casually or otherwise.

An easy guess would be that Tom had found out about Laura through her reputation, the sort of reputation that would have appealed to a man with Tom's interest in sex. In any case, Tom continued to alternate his sexual activity between Ann Melton and Laura Foster through the early months of 1866.

Chronologically, the next noteworthy event to occur in the development of the Tom Dula – Laura Foster murder case occurred the first of March, 1866. Pauline Foster, Ann Foster Melton's cousin, who shared a grandfather with Ann, left her home in Watauga County, which lies between Wilkes County and Tennessee, and came to Happy Valley. She had come, she later testified, to visit her grandfather and to seek treatment for syphilis from Dr. George Carter, the only physician between Lenoir and Wilkesboro. This is the earliest mention of the venereal disease on record.

In the indictment of Tom Dula and Ann Melton, the State contended that the motive for Laura Foster's murder resulted from the fact that the two accused Laura of communicating syphilis to Tom, who passed it on to Ann.

Dr. George N. Carter, 43 in 1866, was one of the wealthier landowners along the river in Happy Valley, owning a large plantation on the east side of the Yadkin, upriver from Elkville. He moved to the area from Ashland, Virginia, in the early 1850's and married Juliette Jones, a granddaughter of the patriarch Capt. William Dula. Dr. Carter served the people of the region for 35 years and was followed by his son, George H. Carter, who practiced for an additional 45 years – a total of 80 years in the area for father and son.

According to Pauline Foster's testimony, the medicines Dr. Carter used in his treatment of syphilis were blue stone, blue mass, and caustic. She was the key witness in the State's prosecution of Tom Dula, and the Prosecution seemed to place more emphasis on her testimony than that of any other witness. At least, more of her testimony was transcribed for the State Supreme Court than anyone else's. It is doubtful that two juries would have brought a verdict of guilty twice without her testimony, especially since Tom's guilt was based entirely on circumstantial evidence. It is important to know just what kind of woman this was who was most responsible for Tom Dula's execution.

When Pauline began her testimony at Statesville, the clerk of court identified her as "a young woman." The *Herald* reporter wrote:

"Pauline Foster, the principal witness against the accused, is remarkable for nothing but debasement, and may be dismissed with the statement that she has since married a white man and given birth to a Negro child."

In her testimony, Pauline stated that she visited her grandfather after arriving at what she called "the settlement," the Reedy Branch area. Soon afterward, she went to see her cousin, Ann Melton, and her husband, James Melton. They promised to pay her $21 to stay with them and work through the summer. The money was to be spent for medicines and treatment for "the venereal disease," obviously, syphilis, under the care of Dr. Carter. Apparently, Ann and James Melton were not told of Pauline's disease at this time. She had, she testified, contracted the disease in Watauga County. Much later, when accused by Ann Melton of having the disease, in the presence of Mrs. James Scott, Pauline asserted, "Yes, we all have it," meaning, as it developed, herself, Ann, Tom Dula, and Laura Foster.

The greatest irony of the tragic affair might well be that Tom Dula contracted syphilis from Pauline, not from Laura Foster, and communicated it to both Laura and Ann Melton. If it had been proven true during the trials, the State's case for a motive of revenge would not have stood up in court. It is a fact that Pauline Foster came to Happy Valley with syphilis the first of March, 1866, and Dr. Carter began to treat Tom Dula for the disease "in late March or early April." It was after that date when Ann Melton told Pauline that Tom had given her the pock (a folk name for syphilis).

Pauline Foster seems to have been more promiscuous than either Ann Melton or Laura Foster. At least there is the record of more men involved with her than with the other two. Under cross-examination she admitted that she had "slept with Tom Dula as a blind," and had slept one night in the barn with him.

Washington Anderson, a witness at the trials, testified that Pauline spent the night with him and Tom Dula in the woods. Thomas Foster, Ann's brother, stated that he slept at James Melton's with Pauline part of the Friday night when Laura disappeared. And Ann Melton accused Pauline of having "improper intimacy" with her own brother (Sam?), which she denied.

There is enough evidence in these few references to indicate that Pauline Foster was indeed depraved, immoral, and promiscuous. Furthermore, she may also have been an alcoholic. Ann Melton called her a "drunken fool" once, when they had a fight, and Wilson Foster testified that Pauline had offered to find his mare, which had disappeared the day Laura Foster left home, for a quart of liquor. Finally, Pauline did not seem to have much common sense regarding a matter as serious as Laura Foster's murder; either that, or she was drunk when she made a remark to Jack Adkins and Ben Ferguson, local deputies, that she and Dula had murdered Laura Foster.

After Laura's body was finally found, and when Pauline realized that she was in deep trouble, she did not hesitate to turn State's evidence and to tell all she knew about the case, involving not only Tom Dula, but her cousin Ann Melton as well. Such was the character and morality of the State's key witness during Tom Dula's two murder trials.

After the middle of March, 1866, Tom Dula began to visit Laura Foster regularly, walking up the river to Wilson Foster's house at least once a week. Frequently, he would spend the night, sleeping with Laura, apparently with no objection from her father. The climax of this relationship came when Tom visited Dr. Carter in late March or early April with syphilis in its primary state – the appearance of a chancre – and requested treatment. (A chancre is an ulcer that appears on the penis.) The typical medicines for the disease in the mid-nineteenth century were potassium, iodine, or mercury, although, according to Pauline, Dr. Carter treated Ann Melton with blue stone, blue mass, and caustic.

Approximately 21 days pass after one contracts syphilis before a chancre appears. Tom Dula had apparently been having sexual relations with Laura Foster for several weeks before mid-March, 1866. However, Pauline Foster arrived in Happy Valley the first of March with the disease in its primary state. Assuming it was at least a week or more before Dula was exposed to Pauline's disease, late March or early April would have indicated the lapse of a reasonable period of time for Tom's chancre to appear. These facts lend credence to my theory that Pauline initially communicated the venereal disease to Tom Dula, from whom both Laura Foster and Ann Melton contracted it, although Tom told Dr. Carter he had caught the disease from Laura Foster.

On Sunday, May 13, Tom Dula stopped at the home of R.D. Hall, a neighbor, on his way from "preaching," and told Hall that he was diseased and intended to "put through" the one who had diseased him. "Put through" was a regional term meaning "to kill." Hall responded by saying, "Tom, I wouldn't do that."

17

On Sunday, May 20, Tom Dula visited Laura Foster for about an hour, talking with her. The following Wednesday, he returned to the Foster home to visit again. Wilson Foster was away when he arrived but returned around noon to find Tom and Laura sitting close together by the open fireplace talking. Tom left before the noon meal and was later seen by Betsy Scott three miles from the Foster home, walking down the river road.

The next day, May 24, Ann Melton told Pauline Foster that Tom had given her the "pock" and that he had contracted it from Laura Foster. Ann said that her husband, James Melton, also had it and she intended to "fool him and have her revenge too." She said that she would "have do" with her husband and make him think that he had given her the disease. She also said that she was going to kill Laura Foster and if she, Pauline, left home that day or talked about what Ann had said to anybody, she would kill her, too.

After this talk, Ann left her house. A little later, Tom Dula came to the Melton home from the direction of "the ridge road," the way Ann had gone. He told Pauline he wanted some alum for sores on his mouth. He said he had met Ann up on the ridge, and she had told him he could get the alum at her house, from Pauline. He also asked to borrow a canteen. When Pauline gave him the alum and canteen, he left.

Later that same morning, Thursday, May 24, Tom visited Lotty Foster and borrowed a mattock, a heavy tool for digging. Thomas Foster, Lotty's oldest son and Ann's brother, was at home and heard Tom say he "wanted to work some devilment out of himself." Tom took the mattock and started down the path along Reedy Branch in the direction of his home. Shortly thereafter, Martha Gilbert saw Tom "skelping" (digging) with the borrowed mattock along the path near the branch and about 100 yards upstream from his mother's house. It developed later from testimony during the trials that the spot where Tom Dula was digging was only about "two or three hundred yards" from where Laura Foster's grave was later discovered. Martha Gilbert asked Tom what he was doing, and he replied that he was making the road wider so he could walk it more safely at night.

Carson Dula, a witness at the trials, came to James Melton's house around 10:00 a.m. that same Thursday and brought the canteen Tom had borrowed, filled with liquor, leaving it. When Pauline returned at noon from the corn field where she had been working, she found the liquor left by Carson Dula. After the noon meal (called dinner by country folk), Ann Melton took a drink of the liquor and said the canteen was for Tom Dula. Then Ann left the house, carrying the canteen. She went directly to her mother's home with it. Tom Dula returned to Lotty Foster's house a little later in the afternoon without the mattock, and he and Ann Melton left together around 3:00 p.m.

Ann was gone from home for the rest of that day and the following night. Washington Anderson, a neighbor, visited James Melton's house for about two hours that evening. He found James Melton, Jonathan Gilbert, and Pauline Foster at Melton's but Ann Melton was absent. All information as to where Tom Dula and Ann Melton were and what they did the night of Thursday, May 24, and Friday morning, May 25, they took to their graves with them.

Ann Melton returned home "an hour before daybreak" on Friday, May 25, undressed and got into bed with Pauline Foster. She told Pauline that she, her mother, and Tom Dula "had laid out all night and drunk from the canteen of liquor." When Pauline got up to prepare breakfast, she found that Ann's dress and shoes were wet. While Pauline and James Melton were eating breakfast, Washington Anderson came in and stayed "a few minutes." He noticed that Ann's shoes were wet but did not see her dress.

Ann was in bed when Pauline left to help plant corn. Before she had gone far, she saw that the cows had come home. (Cattle ranged free in western North Carolina then, and crops were fenced in.) She returned to the house for a milk pail. When she entered the house, she found Tom Dula bending over Ann Melton's bed, in low conversation with her. Tom asked Pauline what she intended to do that day. When Pauline replied that she "would drop corn" (to be covered by someone else with a hoe, a method of planting), he said it was too hot to work.

On Thursday evening, May 24, Wilson Foster went to bed, leaving Laura up. An hour before daybreak on Friday, May 25, Laura got up from her bed and went outside for a short while. (The sun rises at 6:35 EST on May 25 at that latitude.) She apparently had a conference with Tom Dula while outside. She came back into the house, took some of her clothes out of a closet, and made them into a bundle. Soon thereafter, she left the house again, and mounted her father's mare, which was tethered nearby. She headed down the path from her house toward the Yadkin River, turning north on the river road toward Elkville, which was five miles away, in Wilkes County. She carried the bundle of clothes in her lap atop the mare.

About a mile from home, Laura encountered Betsy Scott, a wash woman, near A. Scott's house. Laura and Betsy Scott had talked two or three days earlier about Laura and Tom Dula. Laura had confided in her, telling Betsy that Tom Dula intended to marry her.

That morning, Betsy Scott asked Laura whether Tom had come to see her, and Laura answered that Tom had come just before day. When Betsy asked Laura where Tom was, Laura explained that he had gone around "to flank Manda Barnes' house." Betsy commented that if she were in Laura's place, she would have been "farther along the road by that time of day." Laura replied that she had started as soon as she could.

When Betsy Scott asked her where she planned to meet Tom, Laura told her that she would meet him at the Bates place. Laura left her then and continued on down the river in the direction of Elkville and the Bates place beyond. She was never seen alive again.

That same Friday morning, May 25, after Tom Dula left Wilson Foster's house, he walked northward along a footpath which paralleled the river road, heading in the same direction Laura followed on the mare. The distance from Wilson Foster's house to the Bates place by way of the river road and the Stony Fork Road was six miles; by way of the path Tom took, only five miles. The Stony Fork Road branched off from the river road to the left, after crossing Elk Creek, in 1866. Heading almost directly north, it crossed some two miles of hills and hollows, forded Reedy Branch, and climbed the slope of Laura Foster Ridge beyond. The Bates place was in the woods to the left.

A "little after sunup" (around 6:45) Tom passed through Carl Carlton's yard, heading in the direction of the Bates place. He stopped and talked with Carlton for a few minutes. He asked Carlton whether the path led to Kendall's house, then continued on his way.

Before he reached the Kendall house, a short distance from Carlton's, he met Hezekiah Kendall around 8:00 a.m. Kendall asked Tom if he had been "after the woman." Tom said, "No, I have quit that." Tom's trousers were wet with dew, Kendall noted.

Mrs. James Scott, who lived on the same path between Kendall's house and James Melton's, was the next person to see Tom Dula that morning. He reached her house just before breakfast, and she invited him to eat. He sat on her front steps a short while and rested, but did not eat. After a few minutes he got up and left, arriving at James Melton's house just before Pauline returned for the milk pail.

After his encounter with Ann, who remained in bed, and his brief encounter with Pauline, Tom left and headed toward Lotty Foster's house and the Stony Fork Road beyond. He stopped at Lotty's and asked for some milk. She gave him a half-gallon. With the milk, he headed down the path toward the Stony Fork Road and his home. Thomas Foster saw him a little later on the Stony Fork Road, just before the turn to the Bates place.

The Bates place was called the "Old Shop" place by one witness. It probably had been the location of a blacksmith shop in earlier times, owned by a man named Bates. But by 1866, any building had disappeared and woods had grown up, obliterating all signs that such a shop had ever existed there.

Mary Dula, Tom's mother, left home early that Friday morning, May 25, after discovering that Tom was missing from the house. When she returned at noon, he was lying in bed. He ate his noon meal and stayed around the house until around sundown. At approximately 3:00 p.m. Mary Dula left home for a short while to look for her cows and encountered Carson Gilbert and Jessie Gilbert on the path between her house and the Stony Fork Road. When asked by the two men where Tom was, she replied that she did not know.

While Mary Dula was preparing supper, Tom "went out about the barn," she thought, where he remained for a while. But about the same time that Friday, Lotty and Thomas Foster said they saw Tom Dula heading in the direction of the Bates place.

Tom returned to the house, ate his supper, left again just after dark, and was gone for an hour, according to his mother's testimony. Returning home, he undressed and went to bed, complaining of chills. Mary Dula said that she heard him moaning during the night and bent over him to kiss him. He was still in bed the next morning (Saturday, May 26) and did not leave again until after breakfast.

Wilson Foster, Laura's father, got up "around daybreak" on Friday, May 25, and found both Laura and his mare missing. He set out in search of them. One of the mare's tracks was "peculiar" because he had started to trim the hoof earlier but had left the work unfinished, leaving a sharp point on it. In addition, the mare's tracks were easy to follow because it had recently rained and the ground was soft. He followed them past A. Scott's house, all the way down the river road to the Stony Fork Road, and along it all the way to the Bates place. There, he lost the tracks in an "old field."

Foster gave up the search and went to James Scott's house, where he ate breakfast and told of his search for the missing mare. From there he went back along the path to James Melton's, arriving just after Tom Dula had left and Pauline Foster had gone to milk the cows. Ann Melton was alone and still in bed. Wilson Foster stayed there about 15 minutes, then left and visited several houses, inquiring about Laura and his mare.

Wilson Foster returned to James Melton's house around nightfall that Friday and stayed for two or three hours. Pauline Foster, Thomas Foster, Will Holder, Washington Anderson, Jonathan Gilbert, and James and Ann Melton were there. "Everyone was joking and having a good time." Thomas Foster burned Wilson Foster's beard as a practical joke. It was at this gathering that Wilson Foster stated that "he did not care what happened to Laura, just as long as he got his mare back," according to Pauline Foster's testimony, and that "he would kill Laura if he found her." It was also on this occasion that Pauline was said to have offered to find Wilson Foster's mare for a quart of liquor. She added that Laura might have run off with a "colored" man.

Wilson Foster left James Melton's house later in the evening, May 25, and spent the night at Francis Melton's. When he returned home the next day, Saturday, May 26, he found his mare there. The lead rope had been broken, about three feet of it left dangling from the rope halter.

Any detailed discussion of what happened at the Bates place can, at best, be only conjecture. It was the State's hypothesis during the trials that the grave was dug on Thursday or Thursday night, May 24, and that Laura Foster was murdered on Friday night, May 25, the implication being that she was buried the same night. An important question arises in one's mind, however: How did Tom Dula keep Laura waiting at the Bates place all day that Friday until nightfall, if that was when she was killed? This problem did not seem to concern the two juries.

The following scenario is worth considering: Tom Dula borrowed the mattock from Lotty Foster on Thursday morning, May 24, and Martha Gilbert saw him digging on the path a short time later, within what turned out to be two to three hundred yards of where Laura Foster's grave was later discovered. It would have been an easy matter for Tom to conceal the mattock in the bushes near the grave site on Thursday. He returned to Lotty Foster's later that afternoon without the mattock, and he and Ann Melton left together with the canteen of liquor, around 3:00 p.m. Both he and Ann were missing from their homes for the remainder of that day and all the following night. That was a logical time to dig the grave. On May 24, they would have had plenty of daylight between 4:00 p.m. and nightfall during which time they could dig the grave, especially one only two and a half feet deep, narrow, and too short for a woman of average height.

On Friday morning, May 25, Tom Dula would have arrived at the Bates place carrying the half-gallon of milk soon after Laura Foster arrived on her father's mare. (Although Tom had a mile less to cover than Laura and had left her house before she had, he had stopped several times to talk and rest along the path he traveled.) If Tom had killed Laura soon after meeting her at the Bates place, Ann Melton would not have been involved in the murder because at that time she would have been home in bed. Furthermore, if Laura had died that early in the day, rigor mortis would have prevented bending her knees the following night so she could fit into the grave.

One could speculate that Tom Dula had hidden the canteen of liquor at the Bates place on Thursday, the day before, and he and Laura had drunk it on Friday, until she was intoxicated and he was able to talk her into waiting at the Bates place all day. If he had convinced her to take her father's mare and meet him there in the woods, it would not have been much more difficult to talk her into waiting for him all day that Friday.

Tom could have returned to the Bates place just after nightfall. Again, he would have been alone. Ann Melton would have been at home with James, Pauline Foster, Wilson Foster and the others who met there that night. This would have been the logical time for the murder. Laura Foster would surely have grown impatient during her long wait. Tom habitually carried a Bowie knife with a six-inch blade in the pocket of his coat.

The description of Laura Foster's death wound in the indictment indicates that such a weapon was responsible. "A discolored spot with an offensive odor" near one of the trees to which Wilson Foster's mare had been tied convinced the juries that Laura had been killed at that spot at the Bates place and her body carried to a waiting grave farther along the ridge.

All this is circumstantial, of course. To continue the speculative scenario, Tom Dula could have returned home and gone to bed after the murder. During the night, he could have gotten quietly out of bed and left the house without his mother's knowledge. He might have met Ann Melton somewhere along the Stony Fork Road, and they returned to the Bates place. They could at that time have carried Laura's body down the ridge, through the forest, to the waiting grave, a half- to three-quarters of a mile from the Bates place, according to Col. Isbell's map of the area.

Folklore maintains that Tom Dula and Ann Melton carried the corpse in a sheet tied to a pole, which they held between them. They would have buried her in darkness and returned to their respective beds. Tom's mother found him in bed the next morning, and Pauline Foster said that Ann crawled into bed with her that morning.

Whether one chooses to believe that Laura Foster was murdered according to this scenario or not is of little importance. The fact is that she was murdered sometime after she arrived at the Bates place on Friday morning, May 25, and circumstantial evidence points to Tom Dula alone or Tom and Ann Melton together.

About the time Wilson Foster was discovering his mare, which had returned home early Saturday morning, May 26, Tom Dula arrived at James Melton's house, where he and Ann Melton conferred for half an hour in low voices. Tom told Pauline Foster that he had come for his fiddle and to get his shoes mended (James Melton was a cobbler). Pauline remarked to him, "I thought you had run away with Laura Foster."

Tom laughed and replied, "I have no use for Laura Foster."

Tom left and went home, but returned that evening with his fiddle and played until bedtime. He spent the night, sleeping with James Melton.

Early that same Saturday morning, Ann Melton told Pauline Foster that she had gotten up during the night and that she and Thomas Foster (who had slept with Pauline) had not missed her. She also said "she'd done what she said. She had killed Laura Foster."

THE SUMMER OF 1866

Some of the events that occurred during the summer of 1866 between the time of the murder of Laura Foster and the discovery of her body, around September 1, can be dated and others cannot be with any precision. But the important ones can at least be placed in chronological order with approximate dates. Soon after the Saturday (May 26) that Wilson Foster's mare returned home from the Bates place, concerned citizens began to search for Laura Foster's corpse. Men came from several miles away to help, including my grandfather, John Witherspoon West, 26, who lived on Stony Fork Creek, four miles to the north. My great-uncle, Franklin West, of Elkville, was one of the searchers; J.W. Winkler was another who helped search "for seven or eight days." At first no clues could be found indicating Laura's fate.

Events came to a minor climax a few weeks after Laura's disappearance. Sunday, June 24, J.W. Winkler and his neighbors were out searching and formed a line "like a line of battle." They moved through the woods up the ridge from near Mary Dula's house to the Bates place. On this occasion, they found a piece of rope tied to a dogwood tree at that location. The rope was made of flax, and the broken end matched the end of the rope which was fastened to the halter on Wilson Foster's mare. A hundred yards (Col. Isbell said 200 yards) from the dogwood were two piles of horse dung, indicating that the mare had been tied there to a white oak. Some 15 or 20 feet from the oak, the men found a "discolored spot in the leaves with an offensive order," about the size of a man's hand. They decided the spot was blood – probably Laura Foster's blood. But they could find no sign of her body.

A day or two before that Sunday, perhaps on Friday, June 22, James Melton told Tom Dula in Pauline Foster's presence that "it was reported about by the Hendrickses that Dula had killed Laura Foster." Tom Dula laughed and said, "They will have to prove it and perhaps take a beating besides." Then on Sunday, two days later, the day the searchers found the blood spot, James Melton warned Tom Dula again in the presence of Pauline Foster that he (Tom) was about to be arrested for Laura Foster's murder. Tom cursed the Hendricks family. (It is not clear exactly who the Hendricks family were, but members who appeared as witnesses at the trials were M.C., Gay, Leander, and Micajah Hendricks.)

The next day, Monday, June 25, exactly a month after Laura Foster's murder, Tom Dula returned to James Melton's house, then went from there to confront the Hendricks family. That same afternoon, Ann Melton tore a clapboard (covering cracks between logs) from the outside wall of the Melton house, near the head of the bed in which she slept, inside. She made a hole through the mud chinking between the logs and ran a string through it. She then drove a nail into a log beside the hole, tying one end of the string to it and placing the other end of the string, inside the house, in her bed. The implication is that she intended to tie that end of the string to some part of her body so that a tug from Tom Dula, when he returned during the night, would wake her without disturbing James Melton.

But Tom returned from his visit to the Hendricks family just after nightfall. James Melton had gone to bed but not to sleep. Ann Melton and Pauline Foster were still up. Tom seemed depressed and did not say much. Pauline offered to prepare a bed for him (there were three in the room), but Tom declined, saying he intended to go home. However, he then threw himself down on one of the beds and began to cry. Ann lay down on her own bed, with Pauline between her and the wall. She discovered that Ann Melton was also weeping.

After a while, Ann got up and went outside and Tom followed her.

Soon thereafter, Tom returned to the room and raised the head of one of the beds, retrieving the knife he had hidden there. Pauline asked him what was wrong, and he told her to come outside and he would tell her.

Pauline followed Tom outside, and he told her "they" were telling lies on him (that he had killed Laura Foster, which he denied to Pauline) and he was going to leave (Wilkes County). He said he would return Christmas for his mother and would then take Ann with him also. Tom and Ann embraced, weeping, Tom told her goodbye and left. When Ann and Pauline re-entered the house, James Melton asked Ann why she was crying and she told him that Tom Dula was leaving.

Tom Dula left Happy Valley either that evening, June 25, or Tuesday morning, June 26, walking up the Elk Creek road toward Watauga County.

For hundreds, perhaps thousands of years, herds of buffalo (bison) came out of Tennessee and crossed the Blue Ridge Mountains to spend their winters in the Carolina Piedmont, returning back across the mountains each spring. Over the centuries these herds, following terrain offering the least resistance, stamped out conspicuous trails which first the Indians and later the long hunters and settlers followed west.

A single buffalo trail led out of present-day Wilkes County. It forked just inside modern Watauga County, the east branch following Lewis Fork Creek and crossing the Blue Ridge through Deep Gap, the west trail crossing by the route of Wildcat Creek. The forks merged again a short distance northwest of a locale called Wildcat.

The trail then ran northwest between the communities of Rutherwood and Luxton, following Laurel Creek to the south fork of the New River, crossing it at Shallow Ford, and continuing to present-day State Road 1333. The trail then followed in turn Meat Camp Creek, Brushy Fork Creek, and Riddle Fork Creek. The old buffalo trail and the pioneer road that followed it crossed through the gap between Snake Mountain, to the north, and Rich Mountain, to the south, and joined the Daniel Boone wagon road at Zionville.

Tom Dula would have followed the existing road up Elk Creek, crossing the Blue Ridge near present-day Triplett, reaching the old buffalo trail and pioneer road northeast of Luxton. He would have had a good road all the way to Zionville, North Carolina, and a short walk across the Tennessee line to Trade, where James W.M. Grayson's farm was located.

But before he reached Tennessee, Tom Dula stopped somewhere in

Watauga County for three or four days, changing his name to Hall. Watauga had once been a part of Wilkes County, and most of those who lived in Watauga had family ties with people still living in Wilkes. Pauline Foster's family had moved from Wilkes County to Watauga. Without doubt he would have known several families where he could spend a few days, but why he changed his name to Hall has never been explained.

On Thursday, June 28, in the week Tom Dula fled from Wilkes County, William Hix, Sheriff of Wilkes County, received the following warrant:

> *To the Sheriff of Wilkes County*
> *Greetings:*
> *Whereas information upon oath hath been made upon the oath of Wilson Foster of Caldwell County that his daughter Laura Foster late of said county mysteriously disappeared from her home, under circumstance as to induce him to believe as that she had been murdered or otherwise foully dealt with by certain persons under suspicion (to wit, Thomas Dula, Ann Pauline Melton, Ann Pauline Dula, and Granville Dula of the County of Wilkes). This is therefore to command you to arrest the bodies of said Thomas Dula, Ann Pauline Melton, Ann Pauline Dula, and Granville Dula of the County of Wilkes if to be found and have them before me or some other justice of the peace to answer the above charge and be further dealt with according to law. Herein fail not. Given under my hand and seal this 28th day of June, 1866.*
>
> *Pickens Carter, JP.*

Pickens Carter was, without doubt, the Justice of the Peace in Elkville and held his "court" in Cowles Store and the Elkville Post Office. According to the testimony of one of the witnesses during the trials, a "hearing was held" at Cowles store on Friday, June 29, 1866. Justice of the Peace Carter found three of the defendants, Ann Melton, Ann Dula, and Granville Dula, not guilty of the charges alleged against them. Thomas Dula's name was not mentioned; however, he was in fact at the time of JP Carter's decision a fugitive from arrest as a result of the above Justice of the Peace warrant.

According to Charlotte Barnes' genealogy, Ann and Granville Dula were the children of Bennett Dula III, son of Jefferson Dula, who was Tom Dula's uncle and owner of the land where Tom was later buried, making Ann and Granville Dula Tom's second cousins. In any case, they were never mentioned again in legal papers related to the trials, not even as witnesses.

It would have taken Tom Dula more than a week to walk the serpentine roads from Reedy Branch in Wilkes County to Trade, Tennessee, with a stopover in Watauga County. He would have arrived at Col. Grayson's farm around Monday, July 2. According to Col. Grayson's grandson, J. Luke Grayson, Tom Dula was hired as a field hand. He worked for Col. James Grayson for perhaps a week, long enough to purchase a new pair of boots, having worn out his other boots in the long walk over the mountains.

An interest in the identity of James Grayson and his relationship to Tom Dula is a natural one, since his name is the only one other than Tom's mentioned in the old ballad. Even before I finally identified him, I could not accept the folklore that a local school teacher named Bob Grayson had loved Laura Foster and had done most of the detective work in finding the evidence that convicted Tom. And I knew he was not the "high" sheriff of Wilkes County, as Judge Johnson J. Hayes had written in his *History of Wilkes County*, because legal records clearly indicate that the sheriff of Wilkes was William Hix.

At first I could not find anyone named Grayson among the long list of witnesses or anywhere else. Tom's second trial was scheduled for Spring Term of Superior Court, 1867, but was continued because three of the prisoner's witnesses did not appear. The trial was scheduled for the Fall Term of 1867, but was continued again because three of the State's witnesses did not appear. One of them was James W.M. Grayson (spelled Grason by the clerk), who was sitting in legislature in the State of Tennessee.

A letter to the Tennessee State Library and Archives resulted in the information that James Grayson had been an officer in the Federal forces during the Civil War, first serving in the 4th Tennessee Infantry, followed by duty in the 13th Tennessee Infantry, until he resigned in 1864 because of ill health. After the war, he had become a prominent farmer in the area of Trade, Tennessee, and a member of the State Legislature.

Further research brought me into contact with J. Luke Grayson, grandson of James Grayson, a retired attorney and politician who still retained an office in Mountain City, Tennessee. He was 81 when I interviewed him in 1969 and has since died. Mr. Grayson told me the following version of Tom Dula's capture in July of 1866:

In the summer of 1866, Col. James Grayson was farming at Trade, about 10 miles southeast of Mountain City near the state line. Tom Dula arrived that summer shoeless or almost so and remained "a number of days" in Col. Grayson's home, working on the farm as a hired hand in the fields. He was there long enough to earn sufficient money to buy himself a pair of boots, which he was wearing at the time of his arrest.

Mr. Grayson said that the sheriff of Wilkes County came after Tom Dula to arrest him. This statement is incorrect; it was deputies who came looking for Tom, Jack Adkins and Ben Ferguson, probably sent by Justice of the Peace Pickens Carter.

Mr. Grayson said that Tom Dula had left his grandfather's farm a short time before the sheriff (deputies) arrived. Col. Grayson and the two deputies from Wilkes County proceeded to follow Tom and overtook him at Pandora, in the Doe Valley community about nine miles west of Mountain City, on the road leading to Johnson City. Col. Grayson dismounted and picked up a rock, telling Dula he was under arrest.

Although not drawn, it was probably the gun Col. Grayson carried that persuaded Tom Dula to surrender (a seven-shot, rimfire Deermore .32 caliber, which Col. Grayson had carried during the war).

After Tom's arrest, Col. Grayson put his prisoner on his horse behind him and carried him back to his farm at Trade, where the fugitive and the deputies spent the night. Mr. J. Luke Grayson stated that Tom Dula was locked up in a corn crib for the night and that his father, W.F. Grayson, who was only 12 at the time, guarded Tom. The next morning Col. Grayson and the deputies took Tom Dula to Wilkesboro, Dula riding behind Col. Grayson, his feet tied beneath the horse's belly. During the ride down out of the mountains, Tom tried to escape but did not succeed. In Wilkesboro he was incarcerated in the old jail, which today is a museum. The most popular exhibits in it are the two cells in which Tom Dula, and later Ann Melton, were confined.

Some three weeks after Tom Dula left Reedy Branch for Tennessee, around July 14, Pauline Foster also left and returned to her home in Watauga County. By that time Tom was already in Wilkesboro jail. During the time she was away from Wilkes County, Pauline apparently took a trip into Tennessee for some reason never disclosed in her testimony. It would have been no unusual journey, since Watauga County bordered on that state. Shortly after Pauline had returned to Watauga County, Ann Melton and Sam Foster (perhaps Pauline's brother) came up from Wilkes County to visit Pauline. Ann told her that "they" were talking about arresting her (Pauline) and persuaded her to return to Reedy Branch with her (Ann) and Sam.

About three weeks after Pauline returned to Wilkes County, in early August, Ann accosted her weeping, and said, "Poor Tom, I wonder if he will be hung? Are you his friend? I am. Are you a friend of mine? I want to show you Laura's grave. They have pretty well quit looking for it. I want to see whether it looks suspicious." Ann at first talked of digging up the body, if it did look suspicious, and re-burying it in a cabbage patch. Then she changed her mind and considered cutting up the corpse and disposing of the pieces.

Pauline agreed to go with Ann to find Laura Foster's grave. They went from James Melton's up the ridge past Lotty Foster's cabin, then down the slope, following the path across the Stony Fork Road and across Reedy Branch. From the branch, they climbed the slope of the adjacent ridge (Laura Foster Ridge) until they came to a pine log.

According to Pauline's testimony, dirt appeared to have been rooted up by hogs adjacent to the log. Ann covered the disturbed earth with dead leaves. However, she told Pauline that Laura's grave was farther up the ridge, between some trees and ivy bushes. But Pauline refused to go any farther with her. Ann, becoming angry, demanded that Pauline continue with her all the way to the grave. Pauline continued to refuse. Ann left her at the log and climbed the ridge to the grave alone. When she returned to where Pauline waited, Ann cursed her all the way back down the slope to Reedy Branch.

About a week after this episode, Jack Adkins and Ben Ferguson were visiting James Melton's house. Ann Melton and Pauline Foster were present; James Melton may have been. They were talking when Ben Ferguson remarked that he believed Pauline had helped kill Laura Foster and had run off to Tennessee (or to Watauga County – Pauline gave two versions of the remark).

Pauline replied, "Yes, I and Dula killed her, and I ran away to Tennessee."

Within a few days of this conversation, Pauline and Ann had a fight at the home of Mrs. James Scott over Pauline's remark to Ben Ferguson. Mrs. Scott lived a short distance south of the Meltons alongside the path Tom Dula had walked on the Friday morning Laura Foster disappeared. Pauline had gone to visit Mrs. Scott alone. Ann Melton showed up carrying a club and demanded that Pauline return home with her. She told Pauline that she had wanted to kill her since she (Pauline) had made the remark to Ben Ferguson about killing Laura Foster. Then she shoved Pauline out of her chair and through the door of the house into the yard.

After the fight, Ann said, "You have said enough to Jack Adkins and Ben Ferguson to hang you and Tom Dula, if it was ever looked into."

Pauline retorted, "You are as deep in the mud as I am the mire."

Pauline and Ann then left together and got about 100 yards from Mrs. Scott's house, when they stopped. Ann returned and confronted Mrs. Scott. She threatened Mrs. Scott and ordered her to let the fight and what was said by her and Pauline be her dying secret. Ann and Pauline left again, but got only a short distance before Ann returned again. She told Mrs. Scott she would "follow her to hell" if she told (about the fight and what was said). Ann added that if it were told, she would know Mrs. Scott was responsible.

Two or three weeks after Pauline's remark to Ben Ferguson, she was arrested and incarcerated in the Wilkesboro jail as a suspected accessory to the murder of Laura Foster. There was still no corpse to prove that a murder had, in fact, been committed. Pauline's arrest would have occurred around August 28, or during the week of that date.

Pauline Foster was questioned while in jail by county officials. She finally told them about her experience with Ann Melton when they had gone into the woods so Ann could check on Laura Foster's grave. Pauline was taken from jail around September 1 and was returned to Reedy Branch. A search party was organized, and she guided the members in a search for the grave.

There were several men in the group, and they were divided into pairs, fanning out in different directions from the log where Pauline had waited for Ann Melton to climb the ridge and check on the grave. Col. James Isbell was teamed with David Horton, his father-in-law, who, at 74, was riding a horse. An hour passed without results. Finally, about seventy-five yards up the slope above the log, David Horton's horse snorted and reared, shying away from a certain spot as though an odor had disturbed it.

Others in the party joined Isbell and Horton and began to search "nervously about the spot," probing the ground with sticks. In this manner, Laura Foster's grave was discovered.

Col. Isbell testified at the trials: "After taking out the earth, I saw the print of what appeared to have been (the blade of) a mattock in the side of the grave. The flesh was off the (corpse's) face. Her body had on a checked cotton dress (and) dark-colored cloak or cape. There was a bundle of clothes laid on her head. There was a small breast pin."

Col. James Isbell assisted diligently in searching for Laura Foster's grave and in engaging counsel for the prosecution of Tom Dula. He also drew the crude map of the area, Exhibit A, for the trials. However, he stated during his testimony that he had "no feeling of enmity against Tom Dula and was influenced solely by consideration of public good" in working so hard for the prosecution.

Col. Isbell was one of the aristocrats of Happy Valley. He was the great-grandson of Benjamin Howard, through his daughter Discretion Howard, who married the first Thomas Isbell. On his father's side, he was the grandson of Capt. William Dula (which, ironically, made him a distant relative of Tom Dula). James Isbell had been a colonel in the local militia before the Civil War and was elected a second lieutenant in Company A, 22nd North Carolina Regiment, when that company was organized in Lenoir in April of 1861. He spent a short while in service, attaining the rank of captain during the war, before returning home to serve in the State Legislature. For the rest of his life he was called Colonel Isbell instead of Captain, which was his regular army rank. His Caldwell County plantation was in the area of German Hill, where Laura Foster had lived. That fact might explain some of his interest in the murder and trial.

After Laura Foster's corpse was found, Dr. George Carter was sent for. He testified: "I saw and examined the dead body of a female at the spot where it was found. There was a place cut through her clothes. Taking off the clothes, I discovered in a corresponding position on her left breast a cut through into the body between the third and fourth ribs. If the knife had gone straight in, it would have missed her heart. If the handle of the knife had been slightly elevated, the blade would have cut the heart.

"The body was lying on its side, face up. The hole in which it lay was two-and-a-half feet deep, very narrow, and not long enough for the body. The legs were drawn up. Such a wound, supposing it not to have penetrated the heart, would not necessarily be fatal, though of a dangerous character. If it had penetrated the heart, it would have necessarily been fatal. The body was in so decomposed a condition that I could not ascertain whether the knife had cut the heart or not. The clothing around the heart was in a rotten condition."

Laura Foster's body was removed to Cowles Store at Elkville, where various witnesses examined it in the presence of the magistrate (probably Pickens Carter, Justice of the Peace), who conducted the inquest. J.W. Winkler testified: "From her cheekbones and her teeth and from the dress, I thought it was her (Laura's) body. It had on a homespun dress which I thought I recognized."

Pauline Foster's testimony: "I recognized her teeth and dress. Her teeth were large, and there was a large open space between them. I had seen the dress before it was made up."

Wilson Foster, Laura's father, testified: "I knew it (the corpse) by the teeth and by the shape of the face, which looked normal. I recognized the clothes. She had on two dresses – one store clothes, the other house made. I knew her shoes. They had holes in them which I remembered. James Melton made them. I recognized her fine-toothed comb."

Laura Foster's corpse, after the inquest, was placed in a homemade coffin and carried to German Hill, near where Laura had lived. You can visit the grave today in the edge of a grassy pasture and near a woods, on the right side of N.C. 268, as you travel north from Patterson toward Ferguson. There is a small headstone which identifies the grave.

Pauline Foster was released from custody, and Ann Melton was arrested, as a result of Pauline's evidence. Ann was incarcerated in the Wilkesboro jail on the second floor in a cell adjacent to Tom Dula's, a solid blank wall separating them. Tom Dula had been held there from approximately July 11 until Laura Foster's corpse was found, around September 1, on a justice-of-the-peace warrant – without bail and without the existence of a corpse to prove that a murder had, in fact, been committed.

LEGAL DEVELOPMENTS

Duboth ring the era of 1866-1868, the North Carolina Superior Court met only twice a year, Spring and Fall Terms. On Monday, October 1, 1866, the Fall Term, Sixth Judicial District, opened in Wilkes County at the old county courthouse (no longer standing), Judge Ralph P. Buxton presiding. A grand jury of 18 "good and law-abiding men of the county" were duly summoned, drawn, sworn in and charged "to inquire for the State and of concerning all causes and offenses committed within the body of the said County." Those selected were:

1. A.S. Rousseau
2. A.L. Hackett
3. B.F. Gambill
4. Harrison Hayes
5. W.W. Summers
6. Wm. Johnson
7. Alfred McNeil
8. Francis Eller
9. D.A. Leach
10. John H. Ellis
11. Edward Parks
12. Joseph Speaks
13. W.F. Alexander
14. Jas. S. Queen
15. J.F. Parker
16. Aron Wyatt
17. G.F. Neil
18. John Wilborn

The most important of the "offenses" was the murder of Laura Foster. The grand jury met, with Rousseau as foreman, and found a "true bill" against Thomas C. Dula and Ann Melton. The Bill of Indictment read:

North Carolina Superior Court of Law
Wilkes County, Fall Term 1866

The Jurors for the State upon oath presented that Thomas Dula, late of the County of Wilkes, not having the fear of God before his eyes, but being moved and seduced by the instigation of the Devil, on the 18th day of June AD 1866 (incorrect date) *with force and arms in the county aforesaid in and upon one Laura Foster in the peace of God and the State then and there feloniously, willfully, and of malice aforethought did make an assault; and that the said Thomas Dula with a certain knife of the value of five cents which he the said Thomas Dula in his right hand then and there had and held her the said Laura Foster then and there feloniously, willfully, and of his malice aforethought did strike thrust and stab, giving to the said Laura Foster, then and there with the knife aforesaid in and upon the breast of the said Laura Foster one mortal wound of the breadth of one inch and depth of six inches of which the said mortal wound the said Laura Foster, then and there instantly died and so the Jurors aforesaid upon their oath aforesaid, do say that the said Thomas Dula, the said Laura Foster in manner and form aforesaid feloniously, willfully, and of malice aforethought did kill and murder against the peace and dignity of the state.*

The Bill of Indictment continues, accusing Ann Melton, stating that she did "stir up, move, and abet, and cause and procure the said Thomas Dula to commit the said felony and murder" . . . and "him the said Thomas Dula did then and there feloniously, willfully, and of malice aforethought receive, harbor, maintain, relieve, comfort, and assist against the dignity of the State."

Simply put, Tom Dula was charged with committing the murder, and Ann Melton of influencing him to commit the murder *before* the act and harboring him *after* the act.

The following witnesses from the vicinity of Elkville, the area where the murder was committed, testified:

1. Dr. George N. Carter	11. Bennett (Ben) Ferguson
2. James Melton	12. Pauline Foster
3. Wilson Foster	13. Celia Scott
4. Carl Carlton	14. Betsy Scott
5. Hezekiah Kendall	15. C.C. Jones
6. Lotty Foster	16. Docia Witherspoon
7. Thomas Foster	17. Carson Dula
8. Martha Gilbert	18. James Foster
9. John (Jack) Adkins	19. Washington Anderson
10. Drewry Atkins	20. Thomas M. Isbell

All the witnesses were from Wilkes County except Wilson Foster, Laura Foster's father; James Foster, her brother; James M. Isbell; and Dr. Carter. A subpoena issued to the sheriff of Caldwell County cleared the way for these witnesses to testify for the State.

The solicitor (prosecutor) dropped the charge against Ann Melton as an accessory after the fact, leaving only the one charge against her – that she influenced Tom Dula to commit the murder.

The preliminaries having been settled, Thomas C. Dula and Ann Melton were "brought to the bar of the Court in their proper person by the sheriff of Wilkes County (W.G. Hix) in whose custody they were and the Bill of Indictment read to them." After the reading of the indictment, the prisoners pleaded not guilty and placed themselves "for good or evil" upon the County and Solicitor Caldwell, who, for the State, called for "a trial before a jury of good and lawful men by whom the truth of the matter might be known." Tom Dula and Ann Melton were remanded to the Wilkesboro jail until this trial began.

Ex-Governor Zebulon B. Vance, wartime governor of North Carolina during most of the Civil War, was appointed to defend Tom Dula – whether at his own instance was never made clear. His associates during the first trial were Capt. Richard M. Allison and Robert Franklin Armfield. David Moffat Furches assisted Vance during the second trial.

Zebulon Vance's great-grandfather settled in Buncombe County, N.C., in the late 1700's. His grandfather, Lt. Col. David Vance, was a soldier in the War of 1812, but never saw action. Such was the Vance heritage.

Vance was chiefly self-educated, except for a year at the University of North Carolina. At an early age he was elected to the State Legislature; in 1858, when he was 28, he ran for Congress on the Whig ticket, was elected and won a second term in 1860.

As a Congressman he was opposed to secession, but once war became inevitable, he became one of the South's most conscientious and capable leaders.

Zeb Vance joined Company F, 14th North Carolina Infantry in May of 1861, but was later elected colonel of the 26th N.C. (Infantry) Regiment. His first battle was at the Battle of New Bern. His regiment was defeated but retreated in order. His bloodiest encounter was at the Battle of Malvern Hill, in Tidewater Virginia, on July 1, 1862. Soon after this battle, Governor John W. Ellis died and Vance was urged to seek the vacant office.

Running on what he called the Conservative ticket, against the Confederate choice, William Johnston, Vance won in a landslide and was inaugurated on September 8, 1862.

Vance was elected for a second term in 1864. During the final days of the war, Vance and his family left Raleigh for Statesville, where he was arrested by federal cavalry on May 13, 1865. He was held in the Old Capitol Prison in Washington until July 6, when he was allowed to return to Statesville, restricted in his activities while waiting for a pardon.

In March of 1866 Zebulon B. Vance began to practice law in Charlotte, associated with C. Dowd and R.D. Johnston. Tom Dula's future at that time was somewhat less promising; that was the month Tom discovered he had syphilis.

Vance had had no previous connection with this obscure and indigent young man from the hills other than a common participation in a lost war. Vance himself had been penniless in Statesville following his return from prison, and after only a short period of legal practice could not have accumulated much of a financial reserve when Tom Dula's case appeared on the docket of Superior Court in Wilkesboro. Dula had no money to pay attorneys; yet Gov. Vance and two capable assistants worked so efficiently defending him that the case came twice before the North Carolina Supreme Court before a sentence of death was finally carried out.

Folklore has always explained Gov. Vance's dedication to defending Tom Dula by insisting that Tom had served in his regiment, the

26th Volunteers, during the war, but this is of course just another of the many myths like those repeated in Wilkes County even today. Tom Dula's gallant service in the Confederate Army probably influenced Gov. Vance, however. The ex-governor used Tom's war record to every advantage before two juries; even so, that does not seem to fully explain the efforts of Vance and his assistants.

Politics may have stirred Vance's enthusiasm; North Carolina was "occupied" by a federal army during the first trial and members of the prosecution were also Republican "conquerors." Members of the defense were Democrats and losers of the war. However, so many years afterwards, this theory can be no more than that.

The first act of the defense, after the trial began in Wilkes County on Thursday, October 4, 1866, was the presentation of an affidavit for the prisoners, requesting a Change of Venue (moving the trial to another location):

> *In this case Thomas Dula and Ann Melton make oath that they do not believe they could have a fair and impartial trial in the County of Wilkes for the reason that the case has been conversed in said county, has produced much excitement, and the Public mind has been prejudiced against them, to such an extent that an impartial and unbiased Jury could not be obtained in said County.*

In response to the affidavit, the Court ordered that the case be moved to Iredell County for trial (in Statesville, the county seat) and that it be set to begin on Friday of Fall Term, 1866, of the Superior Court of Law for that county. This directive was dated October 10, 1866. The Court further ordered that the sheriff of Wilkes County (W.G. Hix) deliver the bodies of the prisoners, Thomas Dula and Ann Melton, to the sheriff of Iredell County at Statesville on Thursday of the next term of the Superior Court of that county.

The old jail in which Tom Dula and Ann Melton were incarcerated in Statesville faced on Broad Street just east of present-day Cooper Street. A pillory, whipping post, and stocks stood in front of it. The jail was very insecure, and several prisoners had escaped from it.

Politics may also have played a subtle role in the transfer of the trial from Wilkes to Iredell County. When Vance first ran for governor of North Carolina, he won by a landslide in Wilkes. But by the time he ran for a second term in 1864, the people of Wilkes were growing weary of the war. All Vance could promise was more "blood, sweat, and tears"; whereas, William Holden, his opponent, ran on a Peace Party ticket, implying that he would take the state out of the war. Vance lost the county to Holden. In Iredell County, however, Vance won by 1,106 votes to Holden's 97. Apparently, Gov. Vance expected an Iredell jury to be not only more lenient toward any client of his than a jury made up of Wilkes County citizens, but also more compassionate toward a veteran of the Confederate Army, one of Vance's strongest defenses.

Captain Richard M. Allison, who assisted Vance in the defense of Tom Dula during both trials, was born about 1824, the son of Thomas Allison, one of the wealthier and more influential citizens of Iredell County, as well as of western North Carolina. Richard Allison was a graduate of Davidson College.

During his early manhood, Allison was county attorney of Iredell, and during the war he was captain of a company of cavalry. After the war he resumed his law practice.

Robert Franklin Armfield, who assisted the Defense during the first trial of Tom Dula, was born in Greensboro on July 9, 1829. He graduated from Trinity College (later Duke University). After studying law, he was admitted to the bar in 1845 and began to practice in Yadkinville in Yadkin County.

Allison enlisted in the Confederate Army in 1861, serving as lieutenant colonel in the 28th Regiment. After the war he moved to Statesville and returned to law practice. He was State Solicitor for the Sixth Judicial District in 1862, while on furlough from the army. After the Dula trial he became a member of the State Senate, serving as president in 1874. His career continued in politics until his retirement in 1895.

Walter Pharr Caldwell, who prosecuted Tom Dula, was born in Charlotte. After receiving his degree from Davidson College in 1841 he taught school in York, S.C., then in Mecklenburg County, N.C. He began his study of law in 1843 and, after being admitted to the bar, he served first as a county solicitor, ultimately rising to the position of District Attorney of the Sixth Judicial District in 1866, a position he held until 1874.

John Marshall Clement, Caldwell's first assistant, was born in what was then Rowan County, now Davie, in 1825. He had attended three different schools before he went north and entered Pennsylvania College, Gettysburg, where he remained for two years. Returning home in 1846, he studied law and was admitted to the bar in 1848.

After serving one term in the State Legislature, Clement devoted the rest of his life to the study and practice of law. Early in his career he served in the prosecution of several capital cases such as Tom Dula's, but refused to do so in later years.

Nathan Boyden, Caldwell's second assistant, was born in 1796 in Conway, Massachusetts. After attending an elite prep school and Williams College, he was graduated from Union College. He began the study of law while still in college and was an apprentice under two New York lawyers.

Upon coming to North Carolina, he taught school in Guilford County while learning the North Carolina law code and procedure. Later, he taught school in Rockingham County. In December, 1823, he received his license to practice law in the courts of the state and settled near Germantown, Stokes County.

In 1830 and again in 1840 Boyden represented Surry County in the State Legislature and in 1847 was elected a member of the U.S. Congress.

Boyden, a Republican, was shocked initially by the outbreak of the Civil War but supported the Confederacy with wealth, labor, and family – one of his sons fought for the South. He was important in Gov. Holden's provisional government in the state from 1866 to 1868.

It is interesting to note that all the members of the defense in Tom Dula's first trial had been officers in the Confederate Army; whereas, none of the members of the prosecution had served in the military during the war.

A Superior Court of Law and Equity was opened for the County of Iredell at the courthouse in Statesville on October 15, the Honorable Ralph P. Buxton, Judge, present and presiding. He was the same judge who presided initially in the Dula case, two weeks before, in Wilkes County, also in the Sixth Judicial District.

Judge Ralph P. Buxton was born in 1826 in Washington, North Carolina. He was graduated "with distinction" from the University of North Carolina and later served as solicitor of the Fayetteville Judicial District. Judge Buxton allied himself with the Republican Party after the Civil War. He was appointed Superior Court judge of the Sixth Judicial District by Governor William W. Holden, provisional governor of the state. Judge Buxton held his office by appointment during Tom Dula's first trial, but was later elected to the same office. He was said by his biographer to be a "safe rather than a brilliant jurist, not that he was mentally slow and plodding but constitutionally careful and accurate."

The Statesville courthouse in which Tom Dula was tried stood on the public square. The courtroom was on the first story, its floor constructed of brick and tiles. County offices were on the second floor. It was later torn down and replaced by another courthouse.

A transcript of the activity which had occurred in the Wilkes County Superior Court, in every particular, including the Bill of Indictment and other details, was presented to the Court in Statesville. The first order of the Court was that the sheriff of Iredell County (William F. Wasson) summon a special venue of one hundred freeholders (land owners) to appear on Friday morning (Oct. 19) at half-past 10 o'clock to serve in the case. The following jurymen were selected and served during the trial:

1. J.A. McFarland
2. John S. Morrison
3. Edwin Falls
4. John A. Haynes
5. William Clark
6. George W. Webber
7. Thomas Davidson
8. A.C. Sharpe
9. S.J. Brown
10. Wm. A. Morris
11. John C. Barkley
12. Jacob Parker

The first motion of the Defense when the trial began was for "severance in the case" – that is that Tom Dula and Ann Melton be tried separately, Tom's trial coming first. This the court granted in response to the following affidavit:

> *In this case Thomas Dula maketh oath that he cannot have a fair and impartial trial, if tried jointly with his co-defendant, Ann Melton, for the reason that as he is informed and believes there are important confessions of his co-defendant Ann Melton which will be given in evidence in this case if there is a joint trial and which confessing will greatly prejudice the minds of the Jury against this applicant.*

Ann Melton remained in jail from her incarceration in Wilkesboro around September 1, 1866, throughout the almost two years of legal maneuvering in Statesville, until her own trial back in Wilkesboro during the Fall Term of Superior Court, 1868. She was present in the courtroom during the two trials but was never allowed to testify, although statements she had made to witnesses regarding the murder of Laura Foster were placed in evidence. From the severance of their cases on, Tom Dula faced the jury alone.

In his opening statement, Solicitor Caldwell announced that he expected to prove the charges against Tom Dula by circumstantial evidence; that he expected to show that a criminal intimacy had existed between Tom Dula and Laura Foster, the deceased young girl; also between the prisoner and Ann Melton, a married woman who was the wife of James Melton. He expected to show further that the prisoner had contracted a venereal disease from the deceased and had communicated it to Mrs. Ann Melton; that he had uttered threats against the deceased because of the disease.

The solicitor added here the details of the Friday morning on which Laura Foster disappeared and the activities of Tom Dula and Ann Melton during the Thursday, Friday, and Saturday involved. He concluded his statement by saying: "By these circumstances and others, I expect to prove Thomas Dula, the prisoner, committed the murder instigated thereto by Ann Melton, who was prompted by revenge and jealousy."

Col. James M. Isbell, the first witness for the State, supplied Exhibit A, a crude map he had drawn of the area where the murder occurred, from the home of Laura Foster five miles upriver in Caldwell County, to the Bates place, in Wilkes County. He swore that the map was a faithful representation of the various locations designated, that he was well acquainted with the neighborhood and had made the map himself, that the various places and distances he had put down were correct, that Wilson Foster, the father of the deceased, lived in Caldwell County, that the prisoner, Dula, and James Melton, husband of Ann, lived in Wilkes County, and that Elk Creek was the dividing line between the counties in that vicinity.

Eighty-three witnesses were paid for appearing during Tom Dula's first trial, but the testimony of only 20 was considered pertinent enough to include in summary, in the transcript that was sent to the North Carolina Supreme Court with the Defense's appeal.

When the Defense closed its case, it asked Judge Buxton to charge the jury as follows:

1st – that circumstantial evidence, to authorize the jury to convict upon it, must be at least as strong as the positive and direct testimony of one credible witness.

2nd – that the circumstances proved must exclude every other hypothesis.

3rd – that the evidence must convince the jury of the prisoner's guilt beyond a reasonable doubt.

4th – that unless they are satisfied that there was a conspiracy between the prisoner and Ann Melton and that they acted in concert in the perpetration of the homicide nothing that she said or did not in the presence of the prisoner is any evidence against the prisoner.

5th – that if they are satisfied that there was no conspiracy between the prisoner and Ann Melton and that they acted in concert in the perpetration of the homicide, then nothing done or said by Ann Melton not in the presence of the prisoner would be evidence against the prisoner except acts done in the furtherance of the common design and declaration accompanying such acts.

These instructions were given as requested, in Judge Buxton's charge to the jury. The trial had lasted all day Friday, October 19 and all day Saturday, October 20. The jury was not charged until after midnight and deliberated all night. At daybreak on Sunday, October 21, it brought back to the Court a verdict of guilty.

Upon the reading of the verdict, Defense moved for *Venire de Novo* for the error in the court in admitting the evidence excepted to in the trial. The rule was granted. Then Defense made a motion in Arrest of Judgment (the act of staying a judgment or refusing to render judgment in an action at law and in criminal cases, after verdict, for some matter intrinsic appearing on the face of the record which would render the judgment, if given, erroneous or reversible) on the following grounds:

1st – For a defect in the record, stating the prisoner and Ann Melton was arraigned together, whereas the word *with* is used in the singular manner, thus showing but one of the accused has pleaded to the Judgment.

2nd – Objection to Bill of Indictment. It is not specified in the body of the bill that the offense is alleged to

have been committed in the State of North Carolina.
The name of the State appears only in the caption.

Motion of Arrest of Judgment was overruled, and at 8:00 a.m. Sunday, October 21, Judge Buxton sentenced Tom Dula to be taken to the "jail of Iredell County, whence he came, there to remain until the 9th day of November, 1866, and on that day be taken by the sheriff of said county, to the place of public execution between the hours of 10 o'clock a.m. and 4 o'clock p.m. and there hanged by the neck until he be dead. From which judgment the said Thomas Dula makes an appeal to the Supreme Court, and it appearing to the satisfaction of the Court here that the said Thomas Dula is insolvent, the said Thomas Dula is allowed to appeal without security."

There were only three members of the North Carolina Supreme Court from 1866-1868. From June, 1866, through June, 1868, the same justices studied and passed opinion on both of Tom Dula's trials. They were Chief Justice Richard Mumford Pearson (1805- 1878), and associate justices William Horn Battle (1802-1878) and Edwin Godwin Reade (1812-1894). Sion Hart Rogers (1825-1874) was state attorney general during this time.

Since there was no secretary who recorded verbatim testimony during the trial in 1866, C.L. Summers, the clerk of court during the Statesville trials, and Judge Buxton would have collaborated in writing a condensed brief of the more pertinent testimonies by witnesses presented before the jury at the first trial. Using the statements of only 20 of the witnesses, they wrote the brief in longhand, which they sent to the Supreme Court with the prisoner's appeal.

The decision of the North Carolina Supreme Court to rule for a new trial results mainly from Defense's second and third exceptions: allowing the jury to hear Betsy Scott's testimony as to what the deceased had told her about Tom Dula having left her earlier that morning to travel to the Bates place by another road and that he intended to meet her there – this testimony was not admissible into evidence before the jury against the prisoner.

Tom Dula and Ann Melton waited in the Statesville jail throughout the remainder of the fall of 1866 and the winter of 1867. Spring Term of the 1867 Supreme Court, Sixth Judicial District, began on the seventh Monday after the last Monday in February, April 15, 1867, the Honorable Robert B. Gelliam, Judge, present and presiding. As occurred during the Fall Term of 1866, 100 freeholders were summoned for jury duty, to appear the following Wednesday, April 17, at 10 o'clock.

Again, Tom Dula's case was the first on the docket. However, Defense presented a motion that the case be continued upon affidavit because three of the Prisoner's witnesses failed to appear. Judge Gelliam allowed the request, and the case was continued until Fall Term, 1867.

Fall Term of Superior Court for the County of Iredell was begun on the seventh Monday after the last Monday in August, that is on October 14. Judge Alexander Little presided. At the opening of the trial, the Prosecution requested a continuance because witnesses James Simmons, Lucinda Gordon and James W.M. Grason (Grayson) were called and failed to appear. Judge Little rendered a fine of $80 each against the witnesses and permitted the continuance.

The verbatim reading of the prosecution's affidavit is significant because for the first time James Grayson, Tom Dula's nemesis, is identified:

> *Wilson Foster maketh oath that the state is not ready for the trial of this case for want of the testimony of James W.M. Grason, James Simmons, and Lucinda Gordon; that James W.M. Grason and James Simmons are under recognizance as witnesses in this case; . . . that the said J.W.M. Grason is a citizen of the State of Tennessee and is now attending the session of the Legislature of Tennessee, of which body he is a member at this time as affiant is informed and believes. . . .*

Apparently North Carolina officials tired of dragging the Dula case out longer during scheduled terms of Superior Court. A special court was commissioned by Governor Jonathan Worth (who had replaced Governor Holden) and the order was signed by him on December 13, 1867. A Court of Oyer and Terminer was to try the backlog of cases which had accumulated in Superior Court. The Tom Dula case met this criterion. The special court began on Monday, January 20, 1868, the Honorable William M. Shipp presiding. Judge Shipp's commission ran as follows:

State of North Carolina:
To the Honorable Wm. M. Shipp, greeting

The General Assembly having vested in the gover-
nor the power to direct Court of Oyer and Terminer to
be held for the speedy trial of "persons charged with
capital felonies, crimes, misdemeanors, or any offenses
against or in violation of the statute laws of the State or
any violation or offense whatever of the criminal law of
which the Superior Court at their regular terms have ju-
risdiction: and good cause having been shown why such
court should be held in the County of Iredell, you are
hereby nominated, appointed, and commissioned to hold
such Court of Oyer and Terminer in said county at such
early time as you may appoint...."

The following jurors were selected from the venue of 100 freeholders summoned by the sheriff of Iredell County:

1. Albertus Cornelius	7. R.I. Davidson
2. A.P. Sharpe	8. Hiram Hastings
3. Samuel Dockery	9. R.O. Sendler
4. Wm. Mears	10. Archibald Hoover
5. James Lipe	11. Willis Hooper
6. Eli Bost	12. Dagwell Harkey

The Dula case began on Tuesday morning, January 21, at 10
o'clock. Defense again filed an affidavit for severance – trying Tom
Dula and Ann Melton separately – and it was granted.

Judge William M. Shipp was born in Lincoln County, N.C. in 1819,
the son of Bartlett Shipp, a noted legislator and public official. He was
graduated from the University of North Carolina in 1840, second in his
class, behind his brother. He was admitted to the bar in 1843. Early in
his career, he was a lawyer and a member of the General Assembly. He
was also a delegate and signatory of the Ordinance of Secession, which
joined North Carolina to the Confederacy.

When the war began, Shipp raised a company for combat in Hen-
derson County and served as its captain until elected a state senator in
1861. The following year, he was elected a judge of the Superior Court
and served until 1868. After the second Tom Dula trial, he continued to
serve the State of North Carolina with distinction for the rest of his life.

Primarily, the same evidence against Tom Dula during his first trial was presented during his second. Again, the jury of the special court found him guilty of murder.

Defense again made a motion in Arrest of Judgment, which Judge Shipp overruled. The Prosecution prayed that judgment be made against the prisoner, who was asked if he had anything further to say regarding whether the court ought to proceed in a judgment and execution against him. Tom Dula declined to say anything.

Judge Shipp's verdict was "that the said Thomas Dula be taken to the Jail of Iredell County whence he came, there to remain until the 14th day of February, 1868, and that on that day he be taken by the Sheriff of said County to the place of public execution of said County between the hours of 10 o'clock a.m. and 4 o'clock p.m. and there be hanged by the neck until he be dead: from the said Judgment the said Thomas Dula prayed an appeal to the Supreme Court, and it appearing to the satisfaction of the Court here that the said Thomas Dula is insolvent the said Thomas Dula is allowed to appeal without security."

After reviewing Judge Shipp's written information of the Dula case tried by the Court of Oyer and Terminer, the State Supreme Court ruled they found no error and the verdict of death by hanging should stand. But by this time, the execution date of February 14, 1868, had passed.

At the Spring Term of the Superior Court of Iredell County, April 13, 1868, Judge Anderson Mitchell set a new date for Tom Dula's execution, May 1, 1868.

The murder of Laura Foster and trials of Tom Dula had aroused national attention, even in those troubled times during Reconstruction of the South. Not only did state newspapers carry stories of events related to the case, but the New York *Herald* sent a reporter to cover Tom's execution. Since he was an eyewitness to the final hours of Tom Dula, the reporter's entire story will be printed in the section of Supplementary Material at the end of this book. but a few details from it need to be included here. The article was telegraphed to the *Herald* the same day Tom Dula was hanged and appeared in that paper the next day, May 2. It covers, when typed, nine double-spaced pages. It was republished in the Salisbury *Watchman and Old North State* on May 8.

According to the *Herald* reporter, Tom Dula laughed and joked when he spoke of his approaching execution during his last night in jail, "exhibiting a shocking indifference to the hereafter." He initially refused spiritual comfort from attending clergymen.

During the evening of April 30, his sister, Eliza, and her husband, who had come with a wagon to return Tom's body to Happy Valley for burial, sent him a note from his mother, Mary Dula, pleading with him to confess the truth for her sake so she could be satisfied as to guilt or innocence. But he said nothing. His sister and her husband requested to see him, but were refused. He remained defiant and showed no sign of repentance and "seemed to have some hope of escape." Those in attendance expected a late confession that might exonerate or implicate Ann Melton, but Tom refused, leaving the impression that she was not guilty.

Tom Dula ate a "hearty supper, laughed, and spoke lightly." However, before the jailer left, he discovered that Tom's (leg) shackles were loose, a link in the chain having been "filed through with a piece of window glass which was found concealed in his bed." While the chain was being replaced, Tom "glared savagely," but said in a "jocular manner" the chain had been cut for a month.

After he had been left alone for the night by the jailer, Tom requested that Mr. Allison, one of his counsels, be sent for. He charged Allison "with the strictest injunctions" to keep the matter secret while he (Tom) still lived, handing him a note "written in a crude manner with a pencil":

Statement of Thomas C. Dula – I declare that I am the only person that had any hand in the murder of Laura Foster.

April 30, 1868

Besides this, he had written a lengthy statement about his life with no reference to the murder and exhorted young men to live virtuously and not be led astray by vice as he had been. The document covered 15 pages.

All indications had been, up to that time, that Tom Dula was illiterate, although he did attend school as a child for three months. He had signed his Pledge of Allegiance when leaving military prison with "his mark," an X with the signature of a witness beside it. The *Herald* reporter did not reveal whether the note exonerating Ann Melton and the 15 pages about his life were actually written *by* Tom Dula or whether he dictated them to someone who wrote them down for him. He might not have known, although his use of the words "in a crude manner with a pencil" seems to imply that Tom himself had written them. There is a remote possibility that Tom, during his long two years of incarceration, had learned to write in a "crude manner."

Left alone in his cell the last night of his life, Tom Dula's defiance began to disappear. He nervously paced the floor as far as his leg chains would reach. He made unsuccessful attempts to sleep, but in vain except for a fitful half-hour. He was still awake to greet his last sunrise. After breakfast, he sent for "spiritual advisers" and seemed for the first time to make an attempt to pray, still denying his guilt or any knowledge of the murder. Early in the morning he was baptized by a Methodist clergyman and "engaged fervently in praying." When left alone again, he was heard speaking incoherently, mentioning the murder occasionally, but nothing he said was intelligible. In this manner Tom Dula spent his last hours in his prison cell.

By 11:00 a.m. "a dense crowd of people thronged the streets, an unusual number of them being women." Many men with "a bronze complexion, rustic attire, and a quid of tobacco in their mouths" were obviously from the hill country where Tom Dula had lived. The execution was conducted by Sheriff William F. Wasson, who did a sorry job of preparing a gallows, which was "constructed of native pine" and erected near the railroad in an old field, since there was no place for a public execution in Statesville. Guards were summoned to control the crowd and to preserve order; saloons were closed. Members of the crowd approached the gallows and examined it curiously. It was a simple structure, consisting of two uprights about 10 feet apart with a crossbeam on top of them.

At eighteen minutes before one o'clock, a guard was assembled in the town square and Tom Dula was led from jail by Sheriff Wasson and some deputies. Tom was smiling as he climbed into the cart, which was to take him to the gallows and which would serve as the platform on which he stood for the execution. The cart also hauled the coffin which was to receive his corpse.

"The procession moved slowly through the streets accompanied by a large crowd, male and female, whites and blacks, many being in carriages and many on horseback or on foot," the reporter wrote. On his way to the gallows, Tom looked cheerful and assured his sister (who rode in the cart) that he had repented and made his peace with God. At the gallows, throngs of people had already assembled, as many women as men, which was unusual for public executions. The few trees in the area were crowded with men and boys trying to see better. Under every shade they could find "every species of humanity imaginable" huddled together.

The procession accompanying the cart bearing the prisoner came in sight of the gallows. Deputies dashed about on horseback attempting to disperse the crowd to make way for the cart and those around it. At eight minutes after one o'clock the cart was halted at the gallows. Tom Dula appeared undisturbed by his surroundings, but talked incessantly to his sister and others in the cart about religion, attempting to assure her that he had repented.

The field near the railroad depot where Tom Dula was hanged later was known as Kincaid Athletic Field, until the Statesville Plywood and Veneer Company was built at the location in later years.

The noose was placed about the prisoner's neck. When told by Sheriff Wasson that he could address the crowd of onlookers, he stood up and addressed them in a voice so loud it "rang back from the woods." He spoke of his childhood, his parents, and his career in the Confederate Army. He referred to the breakup of the Union. He cursed, invoking God's name in his assertions that some of the witnesses against him had lied. He discussed at length the politics of Wilkes County. When he was told, after his question, that Holden had recently been elected governor of North Carolina, he asserted that Holden was a Secessionist and a man who could not be trusted.

His only reference to the murder was an explanation of the roads and paths leading to the scene of the murder to prove that two or three witnesses swore falsely against him. He mentioned in particular James Isbell, who had drawn the map of the area, Exhibit A, used during the trial. He accused Isbell of perjury, and asserted that if no lies had been sworn against him, he would not have been there beneath the gallows.

This concluded Dula's speech, which had lasted for almost an hour. He bid his sister an affectionate farewell, and she was removed from the cart. The other end of the noose was thrown over the crossbeam of the gallows and tied. Tom Dula stood there in the cart, calm before the vast crowd, and said nothing further.

At 2:42 p.m. the cart was moved from beneath the gallows. Tom Dula fell about two feet, not nearly enough to break his neck, which execution by hanging is supposed to do. He did not struggle as he was slowly throttled. His pulse kept beating for 10 minutes. At 13 minutes after his fall, Tom Dula was declared dead by the attending physician, Dr. Campbell. The body was allowed to hang for 20 minutes before it was cut down. It was placed in the waiting coffin and turned over to Eliza, Tom's sister, and her husband.

The spectators at the execution were not made aware of Tom Dula's note exonerating Ann Melton, who remained to be tried.

Tom Dula's body was returned to Happy Valley, where it was buried. Local folk wisdom had always located the grave on the spur of a ridge across the Yadkin River from present-day Ferguson, on what was once the land of Bennett Dula III. In my first book I had doubted this claim because a local patriarch had written a pamphlet on the subject claiming that Tom had lived in a huge log house on the farm, whereas Col. James Isbell's map clearly showed that he had not, and I had doubted that a well-to-do landowner like Bennett Dula would have allowed the body of a criminal to be buried on his land. But after acquiring Tom Dula's genealogy from Charlotte Barnes and learning that Bennett Dula III was Tom's first cousin, I have changed my mind. Tom Dula's traditional grave is very likely where he was really buried.

Ann Melton was tried during the Fall Term of the Superior Court in Wilkesboro in 1868. Governor Vance defended her. The trial was short and uneventful as a result of the note Tom Dula had supplied exonerating Ann during his last night in prison. The following article appeared in the Statesville *American* on November 5, 1868:

> *The trial of Ann Melton, charged as an accomplice in the murder of Laura Foster, took place at Wilkesboro, at the later term of the Superior Court, and she was acquitted. The unfortunate woman has suffered about two years imprisonment, and if guilty, she has been severely punished, and the gallows would have added little to her punishment. Thus ends this woeful tragedy.*

DENOUEMENT

When Laura Foster's murder and the execution of Tom Dula gained national attention following the recording of the "Tom Dooley" ballad in the late 1950's, a monument was placed at the Dula grave site near Ferguson, alongside the old Lenoir-Wilkesboro Road (State Road 1134).

At that time the land was owned by Sam Jones. Except for the name, the information engraved on the tombstone is incorrect, including the execution date of 1865. Within a short while of its erection, the monument was mutilated by vandals who chipped off pieces of it for souvenirs; parts of the top and sides have been destroyed. It still stands today, incorrect in its information and sad in its mutilation.

Ann Melton lived with her husband James for the remainder of her life. Her grave lies on the slope of the ridge just below where Lotty Foster's cabin used to stand – below the modern home of Turner Marley. She is buried without a monument in the small family plot beside the grave of James Melton's sister, Sarah Ann Melton Walsh, 1843-1883.

James and Ann Foster Melton had two daughters and several

grandchildren. As to the ultimate fate of Ann, one must turn to folklore and superstition. There were tales abroad that she lived long enough to have several more children, both white and black, obviously untrue. The most persistent story concerning her early death is that she was injured when a cart on which she rode overturned, and she died slowly of injuries over a period of weeks or months. But one possible cause of her death is far more disturbing.

Tales persist that she was bedridden for a long time before she died. Though my grandfather died before I was born, one version has come down from him, through my father and mother. He told that on the night she died, Ann Melton screamed in terror that she could see black cats climbing the walls and hear meat frying in hell. Folklore has her screaming that the devil was coming to get her. Since growing up, I have heard the same tale from other sources.

I have heard older natives of Wilkes County imply that Ann Melton may have died as a result of the advanced stage of syphilis. This version of Ann's death makes sense. Syphilis goes through three stages: primary, secondary, and advanced or tertiary. Approximately 28 out of every 100 syphilis patients will advance to the tertiary stage, and approximately 15 of the 28 will die of the disease. In the remaining cases, the disease will become benign.

Those who develop tertiary syphilis can die in one of several ways. It can destroy the heart and circulatory system, the liver, and the kidneys. But the most insidious disorder is neurosyphilis, which attacks the spinal cord and brain. When the brain is affected, it causes a mental disorder called paresis – insanity. Manifestations of paresis are invalidism, loss of memory, lack of insight, violent rages, disorientation, convulsions, and delusions.

Syphilis progresses from primary to secondary and on to the tertiary stage over different periods of time in different patients. Ann Melton contracted the disease in March or early April, 1866, and she died in the mid-1870s: a fairly short length of time for the terminal episode of the tertiary stage of neurosyphilis to develop, but still a possible cause of her death. The tales about Ann Melton being bedridden and her delusions of seeing black cats climbing the walls and hearing meat frying in hell could very well have been manifestations of paresis.

If true, Ann Melton paid more dearly for the murder of Laura Foster than Tom Dula did, during the final 10 minutes of his life.

Ann Melton took her knowledge of Laura Foster's murder with her to the grave, although there is a folk story that she whispered information to someone bending over her bed on the night she died. Today, little Reedy Branch flows lazily alongside the ridge just below her grave and along the base of Laura Foster Ridge, across the narrow valley from where she lies. Less than two miles to the east it joins the Yadkin River. The stream flows as it has flowed for the past centuries and as it will continue to flow after all memories of Ann Melton, Tom Dula, and Laura Foster have passed into oblivion.

James Melton married Louisa Gilbert after Ann's death and lived a full and apparently happy life. In a community which condemned and despised Ann Melton and told dark tales of her evil for years after her death, James Melton's name has remained unblemished.

Memory of the fatal triangle in this domestic tragedy would have long ago disappeared had it not been for the old folk ballad "Tom Dooley." Tom, Laura Foster, and Ann Melton would have slept forever in their graves without markers, and nature would have hidden them beneath green fields.

A PERSONAL CONCLUSION

The justice meted out to Tom Dula should not relate to whether or not he murdered Laura Foster or conspired to murder her, but whether or not his arrest, incarceration, and trial were constitutional and legal under the U.S. and North Carolina systems of justice. Furthermore, we need to concern ourselves with whether the civil chaos at the end of the Civil War, during the control of North Carolina by an occupying army and under the jurisdiction of a recently elected governor, contributed to a failure of legal justice.

To start with, was Tom Dula's capture and arrest in Tennessee legal?

It was not. In normal times, the arresting deputies from North Carolina would have been required to obtain a Writ of Extradition in order to transport Tom Dula from the jurisdiction of the State of Tennessee back into North Carolina.

Furthermore, it was obviously illegal for James W.M. Grayson to assist in the arrest of Tom Dula, to hold him overnight on the Grayson farm, and to transport him the next day on his horse to Wilkesboro, even accompanied by the two North Carolina deputies. Grayson was a citizen of another state, and neither Ben Ferguson nor Jack Adkins had the authority to deputize him.

When Tom Dula "signed" his Pledge of Allegiance to the Union and to the constitution in order to be released from federal prison at Point Lookout, Maryland, in 1865, he should have been automatically under the protection of the Constitution of the United States. However, he was arrested illegally, brought back into North Carolina illegally, and held in the Wilkesboro jail for more than a month and a half *under suspicion of murder*, with no *corpus delicti* to prove that a murder had actually been committed – by Tom Dula or anyone else. Tom Dula's incarceration was patently unconstitutional.

Tom was tried before two juries and found guilty both times, based exclusively on circumstantial evidence. In the second charge of the judge to the jury, he explains that "the circumstances proved must exclude *every other hypothesis*."

As the late Attorney Ted West points out in his opinion, contained in supplementary material at the end of this book, the circumstances presented as evidence during the trial fall far short of excluding every other hypothesis. There were numerous reasons why Tom Dula might have gone to Tennessee and might have done many other of the acts witnesses testified to, which the juries accepted as proof of his guilt.

It is, therefore, my conclusion that Thomas C. Dula was illegally arrested, illegally transported from Tennessee to North Carolina, and unconstitutionally incarcerated in the Wilkesboro jail before the body of Laura Foster was finally discovered, and that his trials and the verdicts of the two judges were blatantly unjust. However cruel and demoralized Tom Dula might have been, however distasteful his lifestyle, whether or not he actually murdered Laura Foster or conspired in her murder, he should never have been arrested as he was, found guilty, and executed.

So far as *legal* guilt and justice are concerned, Tom Dula can lift up his head.

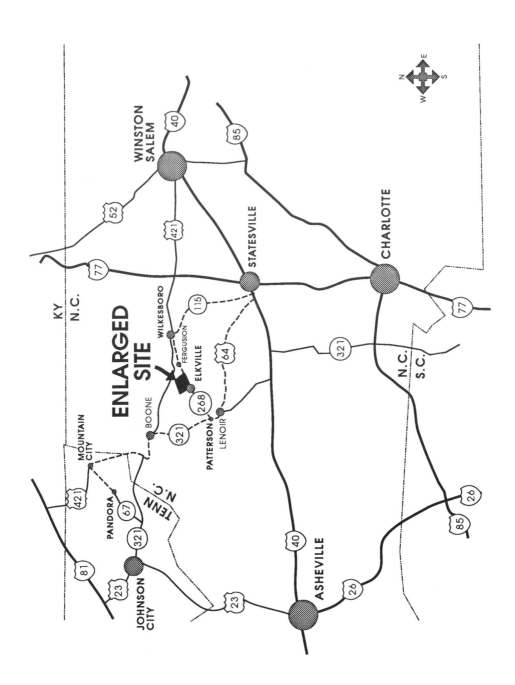

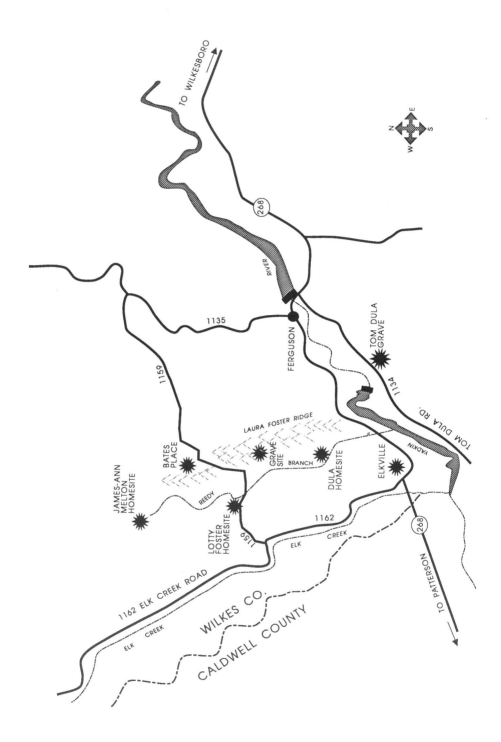

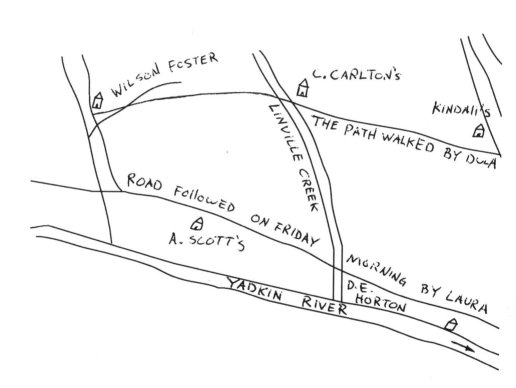

(Verbatim information in faint inscription above)

Path thro from Wilson Foster's to Bates place ....5 mi.
Road around   "   "   "   "   " ....6 mi.
Wilson Foster to A. Scott..1 mi.
Place of murder to where rope was found..........................100 yds.
Place of murder to grave ....1/2 to 3/4 mi.
Grave to path from Lotty Foster's................................150-174 yds.
Dula House to grave..400-500 yds.
From where rope was found in the bushes to
      the Stony Fork road..75 yds.

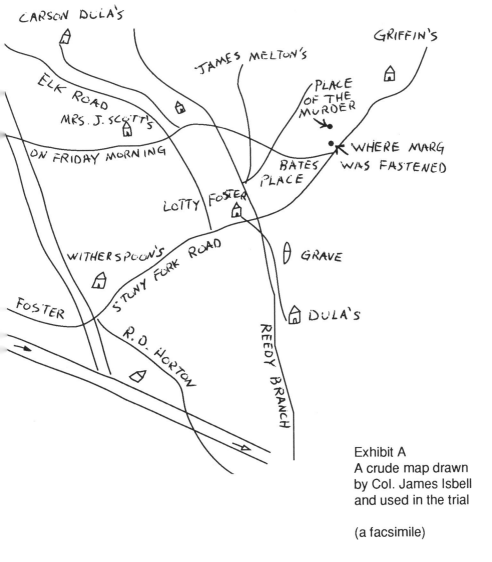

NORTH

CARSON DULA'S

GRIFFIN'S

JAMES MELTON'S

PLACE OF THE MURDER

ELK ROAD

MRS. J. SCOTT'S

ON FRIDAY MORNING

WHERE MARG WAS FASTENED

BATES PLACE

LOTTY FOSTER

WITHERSPOON'S

GRAVE

STONY FORK ROAD

DULA'S

FOSTER

R. D. HORTON

REEDY BRANCH

Exhibit A
A crude map drawn
by Col. James Isbell
and used in the trial

(a facsimile)

Ann Melton is buried in the grave plot just to the left of the stump in foreground. The paved road in the background is the old Stony Fork Road, today called the Glady's Fork Road (N.C. 1159). Lotty Foster, Ann's mother, lived a short distance above the grave plot to the left of photo. (Photograph by John Bramell)

Laura Foster was originally buried in the woods on the spur of the ridge (Laura Foster Ridge) in the mid-background. Tom Dula and his mother lived just beyond the spur of the ridge beside a brook called Reedy Branch, which cuts a narrow trench across the field in the foreground. (Photograph by John Bramell)

Doe Creek, a trout
stream near which Tom
Dula was captured in
the community of
Pandora, Tennessee, in
July, 1866. (Photograph
by John Bramell)

Gun carried by Col.
James W.M. Grayson
when Tom Dula was
captured – a seven-shot,
rimfire, Deermore .32
caliber, which Col.
Grayson had carried
during the Civil War.
(Photograph
by John Bramell)

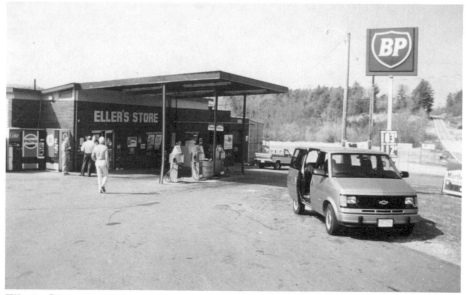

Eller's Store, located on almost the exact spot where Coweles Store and Post Office stood in 1866 – the heart of the Elkville community. (Photograph by John Bramell)

The old Wilkesboro jail where Tom Dula and Ann Melton were incarcerated in the summer of 1866 before their removal to Statesville. The building is now a museum. (Photograph by John Bramell)

GOVERNOR OF NORTH CAROLINA.

Governor Zebulon B. Vance, who defended Tom Dula during both trials and later defended Ann Melton. He served as a colonel in the 26th North Carolina Infantry Regiment early in the Civil War, but was later elected governor and served as governor of the state from Sept. 8, 1862 until the end of the war. (Photograph courtesy of the N.C. Department of Cultural Resources)

Judge Ralph P. Buxton, who presided during Tom Dula's first trial in Statesville, Oct. 19-21, 1866, Fall Term, Sixth Judicial District. (Photograph courtesy of the N.C. Department of Cultural Resources)

Judge William M. Shipp, who was commissioned by Gov. Jonathan Worth to hold a special court of Oyer and Terminer and try Tom Dula a second time (after his appeal to the North Carolina Supreme Court), beginning Jan. 20, 1868 (Photograph courtesy of the N.C. Department of Cultural Resources)

The graves of Laura Foster and Tom Dula. Laura Foster's tombstone is located just off N.C. highway 268, on the right, as one drives north toward Ferguson in Wilkes County. Tom Dula's marker is located just off Tom Dula Road (1134), across the Yadkin River from Ferguson. The date on the tombstone is incorrect. (Photographs by John Bramell)

SUPPLEMENTARY MATERIAL

1. Date of Murder

What was the date of Laura Foster's murder?

The many contradictions in the folklore surrounding this legendary crime are understandable because folklore lives through oral traditions, and the exact truth seldom survives in this manner. It is easy to understand how articles written about such an event a century later can deviate from the facts, how they can be contradictory, since such articles depend on folk traditions, usually information from third- or fourth-generation "experts."

What is not easy to understand is how legal documents with such a fatal bearing upon this murder case could be contradictory in such a simple matter as the date of the murder – or how a contemporary newspaper article could fall into the same error.

Yet that is exactly what happened. In the Bill of Indictment (of Tom Dula and Ann Melton) presented to the Superior Court of Wilkes County during the Fall Term of 1866, the date of death is given as June 18, 1866 – a Monday. At Tom Dula's first trial, in the fall, 1866 term of Iredell County Superior Court, the solicitor's (prosecutor's) opening statement gave the date of the murder as May 28, 1866 – also a Monday.

The first ruling written by the North Carolina Supreme Court gives the date only as May, 1866, and the second ruling the date of Friday, January 25, 1866. Judge William M. Shipp, who presided at the second trial of Dula in January, 1868, indicates the date of death as Friday, May 25, 1866, in his report of the trial to the Supreme Court. And the article published in the *New York Herald*, reporting Tom Dula's execution, states that Laura Foster was killed on May 28, 1866.

In present-day accounts, the one written by Judge Johnson J. Hayes in *Land of Wilkes*, a history of Wilkes County, gives the date of death as January 25, 1866 – a Thursday. Reverend Isbell's date in *The World of My Childhood is Spring*, 1865, and Mrs. Alexander's article in the *Lenoir News-Topic* lists the date as May Day, 1865; apparently she means May 1, which was a Thursday.

The last two dates are so obviously in error, being the wrong year, they will not require further mention. But the discrepancies in the legal documents are amazing, to say the least: June 18, 1866; May 28, 1866; Friday, January 25, 1866 (the 25th was a Thursday); Friday, May 25, 1866. It is difficult to understand why the legal counsel for Dula, whose defense was otherwise brilliant, did not discover these contradictions and use them in the appeal. It is even more difficult to understand why the two judges who tried the case or why the state Supreme Court judges failed to discover such grave errors.

But the important task here is to try to determine what was the exact date of Laura Foster's murder and to support it if possible with written evidence contemporary with the event. Despite the confusion in the legal documents, this can be done beyond "reasonable doubt," and it can be verified from evidence presented at the trial.

These witnesses testified as follows concerning the date:

Betsy Scott: I saw Laura the Friday morning she disappeared.

Carl Carlton: I saw the prisoner on the Friday morning of Laura's disappearance.

Hezekiah Kendall: I saw the prisoner on that Friday morning about eight o'clock.

Mrs. James Scott: I saw the prisoner on that Friday morning after breakfast.

Pauline Foster: I saw the prisoner early that Friday morning at James Melton's house... I saw the prisoner on Thursday morning the day before. (And under cross examination, "It was after breakfast on Friday some eight or nine o'clock," when she saw the prisoner).

Martha Gilbert: On Wednesday or Thursday before the Friday of Laura Foster's disappearance I saw the prisoner.

Thomas Foster: On Thursday before the Friday (of Laura's disappearance), etc.

Washington Anderson: I was at James Melton's on Thursday night before the Friday Laura Foster disappeared.

Mary Dula: Thomas was not at my house early in the morning of that Friday.

From this evidence, one must accept the fact that Laura Foster left home on a Friday morning and was murdered some time that same day. The entire trial hinges on the fact that it was a Friday and that a good many witnesses remembered it was a Friday on which they had seen either Tom Dula or Laura Foster on the way to the Bates place, where the murder occurred. Only one of the dates cited in the legal documents falls on a Friday; that is May 25, 1866, in Judge Shipp's report.

That the murder occurred in January can be ruled out rather easily. In her testimony, Pauline Foster stated that on the Friday morning Laura disappeared she (Pauline) "had started out to the field to plant corn." Further along in the trial she said that she "stayed in the field at work with Jonathan Gilbert and James Melton (for whom she worked) until three o'clock." And at another point she testified that she was "dropping corn," a method of planting used before the invention of the corn planter. (One worker would drop two or three grains of corn at close intervals in a furrow, and another worker would follow, covering the seed with a hoe.)

It is evident, then, that Laura Foster was murdered in the spring of 1866 during corn planting season. Usually such planting occurred in late April but could be delayed until late May, depending on the amount of spring rain, the industry of the farmer, and type of seed corn used. It is further evident that Laura Foster was murdered on a Friday. Therefore, it would be safe to state that she was murdered on Friday, May 25, 1866.

(It might be enlightening to point out that free calendars were not available to the people living in the area of the murder until well into the 20th century. As late as the 1920's, it was necessary for one to walk two or three miles to the nearest store to consult a calendar. Except for the Sabbath, the days were pretty much alike, filled with labor, and dates were of little importance to the average person. However, this does not explain the discrepancies in the legal documents of the era.)

2. Tom Dula's Military Record

Thomas C. Dula enlisted at Elkville, in Wilkes County, on March 15, 1862, as a private in Company K, 42nd Regiment, North Carolina Infantry, for three years or the duration of the war.

The 42nd Regiment, North Carolina troops, was organized at Salisbury in April, 1862. It apparently became a "floating" contingent, being attached to different battalions as a capable reinforcement. The 42nd fought in such sanguine battles as Bermuda Hundred, Cold Harbor, New Market Heights, and Petersburg.

The 42nd Regiment first arrived at Petersburg on May 12, 1864, and was attached to Gen. W.H.C. Whiting's Battalion and ordered into the field along the Swift Creek Line on May 13. Detached again, briefly, the 42nd returned to Petersburg on June 17.

Following four bloody months of service defending Petersburg, the regiment was transferred south again, ending up in North Carolina attached to Gen. Hoke's division, near New Bern and Kinston. There it fought against Gen. J.D. Cox's troops, a corps attached to Gen. Sherman's army.

Following Gen. Lee's surrender, on April 29, 1865, the 42nd North Carolina Regiment was disbanded on May 2.

The army record of Tom Dula indicates that his name appears on a register of Confederate States Hospital, Petersburg, Virginia, containing a list of clothing and accouterments, the letter of receipt dated November 1, 1862; the possessions were returned to the patient on November 24. This record indicates that Tom Dula was in the Petersburg Hospital from November 1 until November 24, though whether from sickness or wounds is not revealed.

However, the 42nd Regiment had seen little action up until that time and was, in fact, on outpost duty, passing time drilling, at City Point and Blackwater, on the turnpike near Petersburg. This would seem to indicate that Tom was sick rather than wounded.

Tom is reported as present (with his company) until admitted to Episcopal Church Hospital in Williamsburg, Virginia, on December 3, 1862, "Re Febris" (with intermittent fever) and remained there until he returned to duty on Christmas Day. In December of 1862 the 42nd Regiment was on outpost duty along the Blackwater River from Ivor Station, 20 miles northeast of Suffolk, on the Norfolk and Petersburg Railroad to Franklin, apparently engaging frequently in skirmishes with the enemy. Tom Dula's fever might have been a relapse, since he had been released from the hospital in Petersburg only 10 days earlier. A muster call dated January-February, 1863, lists him as sick in quarters but present, probably from a lingering illness that had already hospitalized him twice in 46 days. At that time Dula's regiment was in winter quarters at Garysburg, Virginia.

Subsequent rolls indicate that Tom Dula remained present with Company K until one dated September-October, 1864, reported him as "absent in Hospital since August 10, 1864." Again, his ailment is not recorded but very likely was the result of wounds.

The 42nd Regiment had arrived at Petersburg on June 17, 1864, for a second tour of duty there and had remained, alternating with Colquitt's Brigade for occasional periods of rest. The 42nd defended the salient on Hare's Hill, the most dangerous point on the entire line. It was exposed to the constant fire of the mortars, with no chance to retaliate.

Folklore has made much of the fact that Tom Dula was a musician while in service, the narrator always referring to the banjo or fiddle. One apocryphal version has him playing his fiddle around campfires for Gov. Vance. (Nothing was ever recorded to indicate that Tom played a banjo.) The January-February, 1864, muster call of Company K does give Tom's rank as musician, but indicates that he was a drummer. Generally, the company drummer beat out such commands as charge or retreat in battle. The Confederate soldiers did a great deal of drilling when not in battle, and the duty of the drummer was also to beat cadence for marching during drill.

In March of 1865, General Hoke's division met the Federal troops under General J.D. Cox from New Bern, just below Kinston, in North Carolina, on the southeast shore of the Neuse River, near Wise's Fork. On March 8, the 17th and 42nd Regiments left their line of battle during the night and at dawn were on the flanks of the Federals, driving them back. Between 1,500 and 1,800 prisoners were taken, along with four batteries of artillery. On March 10, an unsuccessful assault was made against the breastworks of the enemy.

This charge probably resulted in Tom Dula's being taken prisoner. His records show that he was captured "near Kinston" on March 10, 1865. He arrived at Point Lookout, Maryland, from New Bern, N.C., on March 16.

Less than three months later, on June 11, Thomas C. Dula was released (as a prisoner of war) upon taking the Oath of Allegiance to the United States and its Constitution. Apparently, he returned immediately to his home on Reedy Branch in Happy Valley.

3. Testimony of Witnesses

In reading the following account of the testimony of witnesses taken verbatim from the source preserved in the (N.C.) State Department of Archives and History, one must keep three facts in mind:

1. First, the reader must realize that this is not the complete, word-for-word version of what went on and everything that was said during the trial. It is the opinion of Mr. Newton, the current Clerk of the State Supreme Court, that "Verbatim transcripts probably were not made in lower courts as early as a hundred years ago – simply on account of the lack of court stenographers."

Mr. H.G. Jones, Director of the Department of Archives and History, states in a letter dated 28 July, 1969:

The minute dockets are usually the most complete records of trials, and these were the barest outline in most cases. When an appeal was made to a higher court, the attorneys and/or the clerks involved probably got together and composed a summary transcript for submission to that court. Disagreements probably had to be resolved by the judge or judges involved.

The first trial summary is in much greater detail than the second, which is little more than a precis.

In short, you are reading a summary of the trial of Tom Dula and the barest outline of the testimony of a few of the key witnesses, the few whose testimony was considered the most significant.

2. The entire record was written in longhand, some words carelessly, and many times I had to resort to studying individual letters with a magnifying glass and comparing them with those in words I already knew, when the meaning was not clear from the context. Some proper nouns and legal terms were especially hard to distinguish.

3. I have typed the manuscript exactly as it appears in the original, except for adding an occasional punctuation mark so that a sentence may be more easily understood. Mr. Summers, the Clerk, was careless with his punctuation, and the few commas he used make little grammatical sense.

COL. (JAMES M.) ISBELL

Col. Isbell testified that the annexed diagram marked Exhibit A (a crude map he had made of the area) which was used in the trial, was a faithful representation of the various locations designated, that he was well acquainted with the neighborhood and had made the map himself and that the various places and the distances put down were correct, that Wilson Foster, the father of the deceased, lived in Caldwell County, that the prisoner, Dula, and James Melton, husband of Ann, lived in Wilkes County, that Elk Creek was the dividing line between the two counties in this vicinity.

WILSON FOSTER

Wilson Foster testified that he was the father of Laura Foster. She lived with him. Her mother was dead. He was well acquainted with the prisoner, who commenced visiting at his house two months before the disappearance of Laura. He came to see Laura, who was 22 years of age and unmarried. (He) came sometimes once a week and sometimes stayed all night. The witness had seen him sitting by her side and once saw him in bed with her.

Laura left his house one Friday morning the past May. The prisoner had been at the witness's house the Sunday before and had stayed about an hour, talking with Laura. He had returned on Wednesday before that Friday. The witness had been away when the prisoner arrived but upon his return home, had found Dula and Laura sitting tolerably close together by the fire. This was around twelve o'clock, noon. Dula had left before dinner (noon meal).

The night before she disappeared, the witness went to bed, leaving Laura still up. About an hour before daybreak, she got up, went outside and stayed a few minutes. When she came back in, she went to the closet and he thought she opened it. He then thought she went to bed again. When he awoke afterwards, he found Laura was not in her bed. This was about daybreak. He looked and found his mare gone from the tree where she was usually tied up at night, since there was no stable. The rope with which she was tied was also gone. He looked for the mare's tracks. One of them was peculiar because he had started to trim the hoof but left (it) unfinished with a sharp point to it. He found the track and followed it along the road leading from his house by A. Scott's house to the Bates place. He had followed the track until he got to the old field at the Bates place, where he lost it.

He had gone to James Scott's place for breakfast, then went to James Melton's; he got there around eight o'clock. Ann Melton was still in bed, her clothes off. He had remained there about a quarter of an hour, then visited several houses without hearing anything about his daughter's whereabouts. He had spent that night at Francis Melton's house; when he reached home the next morning, he found his mare there. The rope on her had been broken, about two feet left dangling from her halter, the end "frazzled up."

About four weeks later, he had found the other piece of rope tied to a dogwood tree at the Bates place; the ends of the two pieces of rope had fitted. He knew it was the same rope, since he had made it himself. He found the missing rope about 75 yards from where "I had lost the mare's tracks in the old field. The dogwood to which it was tied was in the bushes."

"I (later) saw the corpse of Laura – knew it by the teeth and by the shape of the face, which looked natural. I recognized her clothes. She had on two dresses – one store clothes, the other house made. I knew her shoes. (They) had a hole in them which I remembered. James Melton made them. I recognized her fine-tooth comb. Before leaving home she had boils about her shoulder. The prisoner never came to my house after Laura disappeared."

In response to cross-examination, Wilson Foster testified: It had been some two months since the prisoner had visited at my house previous to the Sunday, before she disappeared. (My) recollection is not distinct as to the time. When at James Melton's for the second time on that Friday (Laura disappeared), I did not say that I didn't care what became of Laura just so I found the mare; nor did I say that I would kill Laura if I found her.

MRS. BETSY SCOTT

Mrs. Betsy Scott testified as follows: I saw Laura on the Friday morning she was missing. She was riding her father's mare bareback with a bundle of clothes in her lap and was coming from her father's past A. Scott's house, where I met her in the road.

(Here it was proposed on the part of the State to offer in evidence the conversation which ensued between the witness and Laura, while on her journey, as explanatory thereof. It was objected to by the prisoner. The objection was overruled.)

The evidence was admitted as follows: I asked Laura if Mr. Dula had come. She said yes, he had come just before day. I asked where he was. She said he had gone around to flank Manda Barnes'. I said if it was me, I would have been further on the road by this time. She said she had started as soon as she could. I asked where she expected to meet him. She said at the Bates place.

The witness further stated that these questions were asked her in confidence of a communication made to her by Laura a day or two before. I saw Dula on the Wednesday before that Friday some three miles from Wilson Foster's house, she testified. He was on foot.

CARL CARLTON

Carl Carlton testified: I saw the prisoner on the Friday morning of Laura's disappearance. He was on the path which leads through my yard towards the Bates place. It was early, a little after sunup. He stopped in my yard and after a few words with me started off, asking as he left if the path led to Kendall's. He came from the direction of Wilson Foster's and was on foot.

HEZEKIAH KINDALL

Hezekiah Kindall testified as follows: I saw the prisoner on that Friday morning about eight o'clock between Kendall's and Carlton's going in the direction of the Bates place. I asked him if he had been after the woman. He said no, I have quit that. He was walking. His pants seemed wet with dew.

Under cross-examination the witness stated that from Foster's house to Dula's the way he was going, was as near as any.

MRS. JAMES SCOTT

Mrs. James Scott: I saw the prisoner on that Friday morning after breakfast. He was walking. I asked him to come in. He declined, saying he wanted to see my brother, Washington Anderson. He sat on the steps a few minutes and left in the direction of James Melton's.

PAULINE FOSTER

Pauline Foster: I saw the prisoner early that Friday morning at James Melton's house. I had started out to the field to plant corn. Seeing the cows coming, I went back to the house to get the milk vessels. When I got back to the house, Dula was in the house, leaning over Mrs. (Ann) Melton talking to her in a low voice. She was in bed. He asked me what I was going to do that day. I said I was going to drop corn (drop corn in a furrow and cover it to plant it). He replied that it was too hot to work. I had one cow to milk, and when I came back he was gone.

I saw the prisoner on Thursday morning, the day before. Ann Melton had gone off from the house, and he came from the direction she had gone. He asked me for some alum, said his mouth was sore. He said he had met Mrs. Melton up on the ridge and had asked her for some (alum), and she had told him to get it at the house. He also said he wanted to borrow a canteen. I gave him one. He gave it to Carson McGuire and told him to get it filled with liquor. I afterwards saw it at the house, filled.

Under cross-examination the witness testified: It was after breakfast on the Friday, some eight or nine o'clock, that Dula came. The cows were to be used in the field where I was dropping corn that day, since the ground was not all ploughed. It was before breakfast on the Thursday when he was there for the alum. I understand the Bates place and the Shop place to be the same. It is in the direction of sunrise from James Melton's; I think I could have seen Dula that Friday morning while I was milking if he went towards the Bates place. I had got about a hundred yards from the house when I met the cows. I planted corn that day along with James Melton. He had gone to the field that morning before I did.

LOTTY FOSTER

Lotty Foster testified: I am the mother of Mrs. Ann Melton. I saw the prisoner at my house on Thursday before Laura Foster disappeared. He came from James Melton's. He asked to borrow a mattock. He got it and started off in the direction of his mother's house. I did not see the mattock again under three or four days. I sent for it twice, and got it the second time. I saw Dula again at my house on that Thursday. Ann Melton was there also. Dula came after dinner (noon meal), and Ann was there before he got there. Both left about 3:00 p.m.

The next day, Friday morning, Dula came again from the direction of James Melton's. It was after breakfast. The boys had gone to their work. He asked for milk and I gave him a half gallon. He took it and left towards home. I saw him afterwards that day late in the evening going towards the Bates place. He did not speak on that occasion. I noticed two places of a little digging (where digging had occurred) on the pathway towards Dula's mother's house. This was two-hundred yards from the grave. I raised Ann Melton. (It was here proposed by the State to prove acts of criminal intercourse between the prisoner and Ann Melton. The evidence was objected to by the prisoner. The objection was overruled.)

The evidence was admitted as follows: Two years before the War (Civil War) I saw Ann Melton, after she was married, in bed with Dula. I recognized him. He jumped out and got under the bed. I ordered him out. He had his clothes off.

(The prisoner excepted to testimony.)

I have frequently seen him go in the direction of James Melton's, night and day. I did not know where he was going.

Under cross-examination the witness admitted there were other young women living up in the direction of James Melton's besides Ann.

MARTHA GILBERT

Martha Gilbert testified: On the Wednesday or Thursday before the Friday of Laura Foster's disappearance I saw the prisoner on the road between Mrs. Dula's and Lotty Foster's. He had a mattock and was skelping alongside the path with it. I asked him what he was doing. He said he was fixing the path and making the road wider so he could go along of nights. It was between two-hundred yards and three-hundred yards from where I saw him standing to the grave.

When cross-examined, the witness testified as follows: It was about one-hundred yards from where he was standing to Mrs. Dula's, his mother's (house). It was above the old field toward Lotty Foster's.

THOMAS FOSTER (Brother of Ann Melton)

Thomas Foster testified: On the Thursday before the Friday (on which Laura disappeared) the Prisoner came to the house of my mother, Lotty Foster, and wanted to borrow a mattock. He said he wanted to work some devilment out of himself. I saw him with the mattock going toward his home. It was after breakfast that he came after the mattock.

I saw him afterwards that day passing along. On the next day, Friday, after breakfast awhile I saw him coming towards James Melton's. He was on the Stony Fork Road before the turning-off place to the Bates place. This was on Friday also. I saw him again on the same day, about sundown, going in the same direction. A quarter of an hour after he passed this last time, I got a horse and went to James Melton's. Dula was not there; Ann Melton was.

In response to cross-examination: A person passing our house could go to either James Melton's or the Bates place.

DR. GEORGE N. CARTER

Dr. Carter testified: About the last of March or first of April last, the prisoner applied to me for medical treatment. He had the syphilis. He told me he caught it from Laura Foster. The latter part of August or first of September, upon a ridge within one half or three-fourths of a mile of Lotty Foster's house in Wilkes County, I saw and examined the dead body of a female, at the spot where it was found. There was a place cut through her clothes; taking off the clothes,(I discovered) in a corresponding position on the left breast, a cut through into the body between the third and fourth ribs. If the knife had gone straight in, it would have missed the heart. If the handle (of the knife) had been slightly elevated, the blade would have cut the heart.

The body was lying on its right side face up. The hole in which it lay was two and a half feet deep, very narrow, and not long enough for the body. The legs were drawn up. Such a wound, supposing it not to have penetrated the heart, would not necessarily be fatal, though of a dangerous character. If it had penetrated the heart, it would have necessarily been mortal.

The body was in so decomposed a condition, (that) I could not ascertain whether it (the knife) had cut the heart or not. The clothing around the breast was in a rather rotten condition. A bundle of clothes was in the grave.

R.D. HALL

R.D. Hall testified that the prisoner, one day about the middle of May last, at my house as he was coming from preaching, said to me that he was diseased and (he) was going to put them through who diseased him. I replied, Tom, I would not do that.

J.W. WINKLER

J.W. Winkler testified: There was a general search made for Laura Foster. I searched seven or eight days myself. One Sunday, four weeks after her disappearance, the neighbors were all out (and) formed a search line like a line of battle. We searched in sight of the Dula house.

I never saw him (prisoner) engaged in the search. We searched about the Bates – or Old Shop place. I saw a rope near there tied around a dogwood. I did not find it myself but saw it soon after (it was found). The branches of the tree near the dogwood appeared to be nipped off. The end of the rope appeared to be chewed. It was of flax and corresponded with the other end (of the rope bridle on Wilson Foster's mare). I think the rope we found was Foster's. I had seen his mare tied with such a rope before.

Some two hundred yards from the dogwood tree, on the same side, that is the left side, of Stony Fork Road, I saw another place where there were signs of a horse having been hitched. Near this place was a discolored spot of ground, over which twigs had been pulled. The bushes near had been broken off and appeared to be hanging down. The discoloration of the ground at this spot extended the width of my hand. The smell of the earth was offensive and differed from that of the surrounding earth.

I knew Laura Foster. I saw the dead body. I thought from her cheekbones and her teeth and from the dress that it was her body. It had on a homespun dress which I thought I knew.

In response to cross examination: Laura's teeth were large. I don't think there was any space between them. I saw no horse track around the dogwood tree. I think part of the time and most of the time we were searching that Dula was in jail. The so-called blood spot was out of reach of the white oak, to which the horse was tied the second time as we thought. It was some fifteen or twenty feet off from the white oak. I thought the discolored spot was blood. I supposed so from what I concluded was an attempt at concealment. I think it was a mile or three-fourths (of a mile) from the blood spot to the grave. (I was) never at the grave but knew the ridge where it was found.

PAULINE FOSTER

Pauline Foster: I was staying at James Melton's as a hireling (witness is a young woman). I went there for the first time in March last. Dula was at the house. He was there most every day while (I was) in the settlement. He stayed there sometimes at night. I have seen him in bed with Ann Melton, wife of James Melton, frequently. There were three beds in the room. James Melton did not sleep with his wife. The prisoner would slip to bed with her after she had gone to bed. He would first lay down with James Melton.

Ann Melton became sick. The remedies she used were blue stone, blue mass, and caustic.

(Here it was proposed by the state to show by this witness what Ann Melton had said was the matter with her and who had occasioned her sickness. This was objected to by the prisoner but admitted by the court. The witness then stated that Ann Melton told her, not in the presence of Dula, however, that Dula had given her the pock. This was said about a month after the witness went to live at the Melton's and previous to Laura Foster's disappearance. The prisoner excepted.)   The witness continued her testimony: Ann Melton left her husband's house on the Thursday before that Friday in May after dinner (noon meal) with a canteen of liquor, which had been filled for the prisoner, and went in the direction of the Ridge Road. She was absent from that time until an hour before day on Friday. She came and got in bed with me. I left her in bed when I went to work. Her dress was wet and so were her shoes. She lay in bed until after breakfast. This was the morning I mentioned that Dula stood over her and talked with her while she was in bed. When I came to get dinner, Ann Melton was on the bed and remained so until I left for the field. I stayed in the field at work with Jonathan Gilbert and James Melton until three o'clock.

Wilson Foster came to James Melton's about dark Friday night and left two or three hours in the night (after nightfall). Thomas Foster was also there and stayed all night. I sat up with him until midnight. On Saturday morning, Dula came early. He and Ann Melton conversed together in a low tone for half an hour. He said he came for his fiddle and to get his shoes mended. I remarked to him, "I thought you had run away with Laura Foster." He laughed and said, "I have no use for Laura Foster." He left for home. Dula came there again that night and stayed all night. He went to bed with James Melton. Dula was there every day or night after that as long as he remained in the settlement. He remained in the settlement some four weeks after the disappearance of Laura Foster and then left for Tennessee.

(Here, it was proposed by the State to offer in evidence the conduct of Ann Melton the evening previous to the departure of the prisoner to Tennessee. This was objected to by the prisoner for the reason that according to the theory of the state, the murder of Laura Foster was at that time an accomplished fact; which murder the state charged was perpetrated by the prisoner, incited thereto by Ann Melton. Any conduct of Ann Melton after the accomplishment of the alleged crime could not have contributed to the accomplishment and therefore ought not to be admitted against the prisoner, who was now alone on trial. It was also distinctly stated by the prisoner's counsel that they made this objection in advance to the exception of evidence of any act by Ann Melton, not now on trial, done by her or word spoken by her after the alleged time of the murder, as such acts and words could not have been done and spoken in furtherance of the common alleged design. Objections by prisoner were overruled by the Court.)

The witness continuing, testified that the afternoon before the prisoner left the neighborhood, Ann Melton went to the head of the (her) bed and tore off a clapboard from the log side of the house and scraped the dust off and made a hole through the chinking. She then drove a nail in the log outside, put a string through the hole, tied one end to the nail and put the other end in bed. She also put a knife under the head of the bed.

(Here the prisoner excepted.)

Thomas Dula came a little after dark. He waked James Melton and came in (the house) afterwards. We sat up until bedtime. I offered to fix a bed for Dula, but he declined. He threw himself across one of the beds with his clothes on. Mrs. Melton lay down on my bed. I got in behind her. I found she was crying. After a while, he (Dula) came from his bed, which was at the foot of ours, into ours, getting in on the outside from me. I heard them both sobbing. Ann Melton arose and went outside; he followed her. Afterwards he came back and raised up the head of the bed. I asked him what was the matter. He said, "Come outside and I will tell you." I went out, and he said they were telling lies on him and he had to leave. He said he was coming back for Ann and that he would take her away with him. They embraced and parted in tears. This was four weeks after Laura Foster's disappearance.

Two or three days before their parting, I heard James Melton say in the presence of the prisoner that "it was reported about (by the) Hendricks(es) that Dula had killed Laura Foster." Dula laughed and said, "They would have it to prove and perhaps take a beating besides."

(Here the State proposed to show by the acts of Ann Melton without calling her declarations that she undertook to accompany the witness to the grave of Laura Foster and did in fact accompany her to a point within one hundred yards thereof and at that point did cover with leaves a spot of ground where the soil had been disturbed. The prisoner objected to this for the reason alleged in the fourth exception. The objection was overruled and the evidence was admitted by the Court.)

The witness stated that on one occasion after Dula was in jail on this charge, at the instance of Ann Melton, I started with her from the house of James Melton. We went by Lotty Foster's, crossed the Reedy Branch, went through an old field onto a ridge up to a log. Here Ann Melton picked up an apron full of leaves and placed them on a place by the log that appeared to have been rooted about. The place where we stopped was one hundred yards or a little more from the grave as it was afterwards discovered. We were going in that direction (of grave) when I became frightened and refused to proceed.

(The prisoner excepted.)

I saw the dead body. I thought it was the body of Laura Foster. I recognized her teeth and dress. Her teeth were large and there was a large open space between them. I had seen the dress before it was made up. It was woven with a single slay.

In response to cross-examination: I hadn't seen Laura Foster since the first of March. It was nearly three months between that time and the discovery of the body. The heel of the shoes on the corpse were worn and pieced. There was a hole in one of the shoes, in the side of the toe. Laura's tooth was not out, but there was a natural space right in the center of the mouth.

Dula came to James Melton's on Thursday before the Friday of Laura's disappearance before breakfast and left without breakfast. This was the time he got the alum and canteen. Ann Melton remarked when she went off on that Thursday with the canteen that she was going to her mother's. She didn't come back until Friday morning early. She was home all day Friday. Dula came there but one time that day. I didn't go off the place that day.

Wilson Foster, Thomas Foster, William Holder, and Washington Anderson were there at James Melton's on that Friday night. We were all joking that night. Thomas Foster burned the old man's (Wilson Foster) whiskers. Thomas Foster did not sleep with me that night. I got in bed with Ann Melton.

I admit I have this venereal disease. I got it in Watauga County and came to James Melton's to get cured and worked with him for money to buy medicines. Ann Melton is a distant relative of mine. I did go to meet a Negro boy near the road, who was sent for me by Mrs. James Scott. The boy gave me a message from Laura Foster. I was arrested and sent to jail for what I said in jest to Jack Atkins and Ben Ferguson.

I had been over into Tennessee and after my return, one evening, Ben Ferguson said to me that I had killed Laura Foster. I replied, "Yes, I and Dula killed her and I ran away to Tennessee." I told James Melton I had this conversation with Ferguson and Atkins as a joke, and he told me not to joke about such a thing. I was arrested two or three weeks after I made this remark.

I did have a fight with Ann Melton on that occasion (an occasion mentioned in the trial). Ann said to me, "You drunken fool, you have said enough to Ferguson and Atkins to hang you and Tom Dula." I admitted then that I had said it, but had said it in a joke. I admit I said on one occasion to George, "I would swear a lie any time for Tom Dula, wouldn't you, George?" I said this also in jest.

I have been twice sworn as a witness about this matter – once at Wilkesboro and again after the body was found. I deny that I ever told James Melton that it was true I had killed Laura Foster. What I told him, I have stated. It is true that I sat in Dula's lap for a blind, one day when a woman came to James Melton's. Dula caught me and pulled me into his lap. I also slept with Dula for a blind at Ann Melton's insistence. I stayed out at the barn one night with him at his request. There were three beds in James Melton's house. The house had but a single room. Sometimes when I was sleeping with Ann Melton, Dula would get in bed with us also. James Melton did not sleep with his wife. I did hear old man Wilson Foster say that if he could get his mare, he didn't care what had become of his daughter.

I might have told him that I could find his mare for a quart of liquor. If I said so, it was in jest. I did suggest to Wilson Foster that maybe a colored man had run away with Laura, and he said that might be so. I also said that I would sooner have supposed that someone up in her neighborhood would have run away with her than Thomas Dula.

Direct examination resumed: The reason I said I supposed perhaps a colored man was in consequence of information I received from others, and so as to the other supposition -

(Exception: Here, it was proported on the part of the State to give in the acts and declarations of Ann Melton on the occasion of the fight between her and the witness at Mrs. James Scott's, alluded to in the cross-examination. The prisoner objected for the reasons advanced in the fourth exception. Objection was overruled and evidence was admitted by the Court.)

The witness stated: After I had made the remark to Ben Ferguson and Jack Atkins, I and Ann Melton had a quarrel. I went over to the house of Mrs. James Scott. Ann Melton came there with a club and said to me, "You have got to go home." She pushed me out the door, got me down, and choked me. After the fight, she said, "You have said enough to Jack Atkins and Ben Ferguson to hang you and Tom Dula if it was ever looked into." I replied, "You know you are as deep into it as I am." I also said that it was the truth that I had made the remark to Atkins and Ferguson but not that I had done the crime. I went off with her to the top of the hill. She then proposed to go back and make Mrs. Scott promise not to tell it. Went back, and Ann Melton enjoined on Mrs. Scott not to tell anything that had been said during our quarrel.

(The prisoner excepted.)

The Prisoner remarked to me one day that Ann Melton was jealous of me. I replied (that) I did not know how that could be, as I never went into his company unless she put me in it for a blind.

In response to cross-examination: After we went off from Mrs. James Scott's, Ann Melton said to me she wanted to kill me ever since I had said that to Jack Atkins and Ben Ferguson. We had quarreled that morning because she wanted me to milk the cows and get breakfast both. We had got off about one hundred yards when we turned back to Mrs. Scott's. Ann Melton went back a second time, but I could not distinguish the words she used. She said she was going back again to make Mrs. Scott promise not to tell anything that had taken place there. During the difficulty she had charged me with having a bad disease and also with having had improper intimacy with my brother. The latter charge was untrue.

MRS. JAMES SCOTT

Mrs. James Scott (recalled by the State) testified: Pauline Foster came to my house and a few minutes afterwards Ann Melton came.

(Seventh exception: Here, the witness was proceeding to give her version of the difficulty which occurred at her house between Pauline Foster and Mrs. Ann Melton when objection was made on the part of the prisoner, for the reasons set forth in the fourth exception, to wit: Dula was not present at the occurrence after the alleged murder. The objection was overruled.)

The witness resumed: Ann Melton came and ordered Pauline to go home, pushed her out of the chair, drew a stick over her, threw her down and choked her. She kept ordering her to go and used very abusive language to her. She also said Pauline had told Ben Ferguson enough to hang her ownself and that she had said she and Tom Dula had killed and put away Laura Foster and had also said, "Come out, Tom Dula, and let us kill some more." Pauline remarked, "I do say now, and come out Tom Dula, and let us kill Ben Ferguson."

They went off together and both came back and Ann Melton enjoined on me to let it be a dying secret with me not to tell she said (that) she had started out that morning to take revenge and had commenced with her best friend. Ann afterwards came back by herself, appeared to be still mad. She said she would follow me to hell if I told it, and if it was told, she would know where it came from, as but four had heard it.

(The prisoner excepted.)

In response to cross-examination of Mrs. Scott: Pauline said "it is the truth and you are as deep in the mud as I am in the mire." Ann replied, "You are a liar!" Ann threw up to Pauline having a disease. Pauline replied, "Yes, we all have it!" I have seen Pauline sitting in Dula's lap often, and (them) whispering together. Ann was always present on these occasions. I remember that Pauline and Dula came to my house together once. I have seen Ann Melton also sit in Dula's lap.

WASHINGTON ANDERSON

Washington Anderson testified: I was at James Melton's on Thursday night before the Friday Laura Foster disappeared. James Melton, Jonathan Gilbert, and Pauline Foster were there. Mrs. Ann Melton was not there. I stayed about two hours. I went by there next morning. Ann Melton was on the bed sick. Her shoes were wet. I did not see her dress. The folks were eating breakfast.

Cross-examination: The shoes were women's shoes and were by the bed. I could not swear whose they were. James Melton is a shoemaker. I knew the general character of the prisoner while in the Army. I was in the same company and regiment. His character was good as a soldier. I knew him as a truthful man and as a peaceable man while at home, and he was good for honesty.

I remember Pauline Foster meeting Dula one night near the road. I also remember her spending the night with him in the woods. I was along with them.

JOHN (JACK) ATKINS

John Atkins testified: I went after Thomas Dula into Tennessee about a month after the disappearance of Laura Foster. He said he had changed his name to Hall while in Watauga County, said that he did it for fun.

COL. (JAMES M.) ISBELL

Col. Isbell (recalled by the State) testified: I was at the grave at the time of the discovery. My father-in-law (David E. Horton) was with me. It (the discovery) was made as follows: Pauline Foster was arrested and while in jail, gave substantially the statement which she has made here today. In consequence of the disclosure made by her, she was taken out of jail. We went with her to the ridge, came to the log, saw where dirt had been removed. This was the spot where she stated she stopped following Ann Melton. After half an hour's search we found the grave seventy-five yards from this place. The earth had been carried away and the sod replaced. It escaped our observation until my companion's (Horton's) horse snorted and gave signs of smelling something. We then searched narrowly about the spot and by probing the ground discovered the grave. After taking out the earth, I saw the prints of what appeared to have been a mattock in the hard side of the grave. The flesh was off the face. The body had on a checked cotton dress (and) a dark-colored cloak or cape. There was a bundle of clothes laid on the head. There was also a small breast pin. I noticed in a former search we made about the Bates place, we found a rope around a dogwood tree seventy-five yards from the road in the bushes. We also saw another place where there were signs of a horse having been hitched; this was some two hundred yards from the dogwood. The horse had dunged twice. About fifteen steps off from this latter place we found a discolored spot of ground; the earth smelt offensive. Some broken bushes were lying on the ground near (by). They had been disturbed when I saw them. The grave was not far from the path leading to Lotty Foster's house, but it was on a secluded, thickety ridge.

During the search we discovered a large mudhole near Francis Melton's which we intended to drag but it being late in the evening, put off until the next day. The next day we discovered signs of mud leading off from that direction toward the Yadkin River near Witherspoon's. We had not noticed these signs the day before. We dragged the hole but found nothing. No other female had disappeared from that neighborhood at that time except Laura Foster. No other person had gone off from the neighborhood except Thomas Dula.

In response to cross-examination: I think it was about five or six weeks after the disappearance of Laura Foster, before Pauline Foster left for Watauga. She was arrested twice. It was generally reported that Ann Melton indulged in illicit intercourse with others besides the prisoner.

I have assisted in employing counsel for the prosecution. I have no feeling of enmity against the accused. I am influenced solely by consideration of public good.

DR. GEORGE N. CARTER

Dr. George N. Carter (recalled by the State) testified: I have heard Pauline Foster examined heretofore; (I) also heard her evidence on this trial. Her evidence is substantially the same with some exceptions as to matters on which she was not questioned. I observed no conflict in her evidence upon the two occasions.

(Here the State rested its case. The foregoing witnesses were separated, with the exception of Col. Isbell and Dr. Carter. Mrs. Ann Melton was allowed to be in court during this examination.)

(The prisoner's witnesses were also separated.)

THOMAS FOSTER

Thomas Foster (recalled for prisoner) testified: I slept part of the night that Friday night at James Melton's with Pauline Foster. I have seen Pauline and Dula sitting in each other's lap.

J.W. WINKLER

J.W. Winkler (recalled for prisoner) testified: I was present when Pauline Foster was examined at a store in Elkville before a magistrate about this matter. After her examination, she remarked to a person there present, "I would swear a lie any time for Tom Dula, wouldn't you, George?"

MRS. MARY DULA

Mrs. Mary Dula testified as follows: I am the mother of the prisoner. He was twenty-two years of age on the 20th of June last (June 20, 1866). His home was with me. Thomas was not at my house early in the morning of that Friday. I left the house after early breakfast that day and got back just before dinner hour. (I) found him lying on the bed. He ate no dinner and was there until sundown or thereabouts. While I was getting supper, he started away and stayed off about the barn. He came back to supper. He went to bed as usual. I heard him during the night making a little moan. I went to his bed. He had been complaining of chills. He was my sole remaining boy. I had lost two in the war. I leaned my face down and kissed him. I did not hear him go out that night and have no knowledge of his doing so. He was there in the morning until after breakfast.

In response to cross examination: I did not say in the presence of Carson Gilbert or others that Friday that I did not know where my son Thomas was. I met them on the afternoon of that day near Lotty Foster's on the path between her house and mine. I had walked out to look after my cows. In reply to an inquiry made of me, I told them, "I did not know where Thomas was unless he had gone to muster." I did that at his request as he said he was too useless to go to the muster and did not want to be bothered by people making inquiries. The prisoner went out just at dark that evening and stayed out about an hour. He went to bed that night before I did and took his clothes off as usual.

I have a grown daughter named Eliza, who lives with me. I left her home on the occasion of my leaving on that Friday morning. I have no recollection of hearing her say that Thomas had been away all day.

RUFUS HORTON

Rufus Horton testified that he was acquainted with the general character of Mrs. Mary Dula, the last witness, and that it was good for truth and honesty; he had never heard it doubted (that she was honest).

(Here the prisoner rested his case.)

(The State resumed its evidence.)

JESSE GILBERT

Jesse Gilbert testified: I saw Mrs. Mary Dula on that Friday evening (afternoon) as Carson and myself went by Lotty Foster's house.

(Here, the State proposed to offer as evidence the witness's version of what was said on that occasion to and by the witness Mrs. Dula with the view of contradicting her. This was objected to by the prisoner for the reason that this was a collateral matter sufficiently inquired into and that the State was precluded from further inquiry, being bound by the answer of the witness. The objection was overruled and the evidence was allowed by the Court.)

The witness then stated that Carson (Gilbert) called to Mrs. Dula and asked her where her son Tom was. She replied that she did not know; she hadn't seen him that day. (He was) gone to the muster, I expect.

(The prisoner excepted.)

This was about 3:00 p.m. We walked thirteen miles that evening (afternoon) by dark after seeing her.

MARTHA GILBERT

Martha Gilbert (recalled by the state) testified: Along where I saw the prisoner skelping the path the day I alluded to, it wasn't steep. The path was steep and broken further on towards Mrs. Dula's but not towards Lotty Foster's.

(Here the State closed its case and the prisoner resumed his evidence.)

RUFUS HORTON

Rufus Horton (recalled by the prisoner) testified: I know the general character of Jesse Gilbert. It is bad for stealing and lying.

(Here the prisoner closed his case.)

4. Charge and Ruling of the Judge

The prisoner's counsel asked the Judge to charge [the jury]:

1st – that circumstantial evidence, to authorize the jury to convict upon it, must be at least as strong as the positive and direct testimony of one credible witness.

2nd – that the circumstances proved must exclude every other hypothesis.

3rd – that the evidence must convince the jury of the prisoner's guilt beyond a reasonable doubt.

4th – that unless they are satisfied that there was a conspiracy between the prisoner and Ann Melton and that they acted in concert in the perpetration of the homicide, nothing that she said or did not in the presence of the prisoner is any evidence against the prisoner.

5th – that if they are satisfied that there was no confederacy between the prisoner and Ann Melton and that they acted in concert in the perpetration of the homicide, then nothing done or said by Ann Melton not in the presence of the prisoner would be evidence against the prisoner except acts done in futherance of the common design and declaration accompanying such acts.

The above instructions were given, as asked, in the charge of the Court to the jury. The jury, having returned a verdict of guilty against the prisoner, his counsel moved for *venico de novo* for the error in the Court in admitting the evidence excepted to on the trial. The rule was granted. A motion was then made in Arrest of Judgment on the following grounds:

1st – For a defect in the Record, stating the arraignment of the prisoner and Ann Melton was arraigned together, whereas the word with is used in the singular manner, thus showing but one of the accused had pleaded to the Judgment.

2nd – Objections to Bill of Indictment. It is not specified in the body of the bill that the offense is alleged to have been committed in the State of North Carolina. The name of the State appears only in the caption.

Motion in Arrest was overruled. The judgment of death was pronounced upon the prisoner, from which judgment he craved and obtained an appeal to the [State] Supreme Court. The appeal was allowed without security according to the act of the [General] Assembly, the prisoner being unable to give it [security].

There follows here a short summary of the brief of the State counsel, the arguments, cases cited as authority, etc. But this is treated so completely in the decision of the Supreme Court it is better excluded here.

Following is the text of Judge Buxton's ruling:

The prisoner being brought to bar of the court in the custody of the sheriff, motion in arrest of judgment. Overruled and judgment being produced by the solicitor and upon this, it is demanded of the said Thomas Dula if he hath any thing to say wherefore this court here ought not, upon the premises and verdict aforesaid to proceed to Judgment and execution against him, who nothing further saith than he has already said, whereupon all and singular the premises being seen and by the court here fully understood, it is considered by the court here that the said Thomas Dula be taken to the jail of Iredell County, whence he came, there to remain until the 9th day of November, 1866 and that on that day he be taken by sheriff of said County to the place of public execution of said county, between the hours of 10 o'clock a.m. and 4 o'clock p.m. and there hanged by the neck until he be dead. From which judgment the said Thomas Dula makes an appeal to the Supreme Court, and it appearing to the satisfaction of the Court here that the said Thomas Dula is insolvent, the said Thomas Dula is allowed to appeal without security.

And at Spring term, 1867 of our said Superior Court of Law being held for our said county of Iredell on the 7th Monday after the last Monday in February, 1867 [April 15] – the Honorable Robert B. Gelliam, Judge, present and presiding, the following Record was made:

> State
> vs
> Thomas Dula
> Ann Melton

> Special venue of one hundred freeholders summoned for jury to appear on Wednesday morning of the Term at the hour of 10 o'clock.
> Prisoners remanded to Jail.
> Wednesday morning, April 17,1867

> State   Murder
> vs
> Thomas Dula &
> Ann Melton

The prisoners Thomas Dula and Ann Melton again brought to the Bar of the Court upon motion this case was continued upon affidavit of Thomas Dula and set for hearing on Tuesday of the next term of the Court.
State vs Thomas Dula. In this case the defendant maketh oath that as he is advised and believes he can not come safely to trial for the want of the testimony of

the following witnesses, to wit: F.F. Hendricks, of Caldwell County; Francis Farmer and Mary James of Watauga County, all of whom are under sepona [subpoena] and absent without affiant's consent or procurement. Affiant further states that as he is informed and believes all the above witnesses are necessary and material for him in the trial of this cause and that he expects to have the benefit of the testimony of all of them at the next term of this Court and that this affidavit is not made for delay.

Thomas C. Dula

sworn and subscribed before me
this 17th of April
1867 – C.L. Summers, Clk.

The prisoners remanded to jail.

And at Fall Term, 1867 of our said Superior Court of Law begun and held for our said County of Iredell on the 7th Monday after the last Monday in August, 1867 [Oct. 14], the Honorable Alexander Little, Judge was present and presided. The following record was made:

State	Murder
vs	
Thomas Dula &	
Ann Melton	

The prisoners being brought to the bar of the court by the Sheriff of our said county in whose custody they are:

James Simmons, Lucinda Gordon, and J. [James] W.M. Grason, witnesses for the State were called and failed; therefore Judgment ni si was rendered against them for the sum of Eighty Dollars each.

On motion this case was continued upon the part of the State, upon the affidavit of Wilson Foster for the want of testimony of James Simmons, Lucinda Gordon, and J.W.M.Grason.

The following is the affidavit, to wit:

State	Murder	Superior Court of
vs		Law & Equity
Thomas Dula &		Fall Term, AD 1867
Ann Melton		

Wilson Foster maketh oath that the State is not ready for the trial of this case for want of the testimony of James W. M. Grason, James Simmons and Lucinda Gordon, that the said James W.M. Grason and James Simmons are under recognizance as witnesses in this case; that the materiality of Lucinda Gordon as a witness was not known until at Wilkes Superior Court and that a supone [subpoena] was issued at once for said Lucinda Gordon, but that Lucinda is unable to attend court on account of sickness, to wit: Typhoid fever as affiant is informed and believes; that the said J.W.M. Grason is a citizen of the State of Tennessee and is now attending that session of the Legislature of Tennessee, of which body he is a member at this time as affiant is informed and believes. That all the said witnesses are material and necessary witnesses to the State in the prosecution of this case, and are absent without his consent or procurement and that the State cannot come safely to trial without their evidence and he expects the State to have the benefit of their testimony at the next term of his Court and this affidavit is not made for delay.

Subscribed and sworn before me		his	
this 16th Oct., 1867	Wilson	X	Foster
C.L. Summers, Clk.		mark	

State of North Carolina
Iredell County

Be it remembered that a Court of Oyer and Terminer

was opened and held for the County of Iredell at the Court House in Statesville on the third Monday in January AD 1868 being the 20th day of said month in said year. The Honorable Wm. M. Shipp one of the judges in and for said State was present and presided as judge by virtue of the following commission to him directed:

State of North Carolina:

To the Honorable Wm. M. Shipp, greeting

The General Assembly by having vested in the governor the power to direct Court of Oyer and Terminer to be held for the speedy trial of "persons charged with capital felonies, crimes, misdemeanors, or any offenses against or in violation of the stature laws of the State or any violation or offense whatever of the criminal law of which the Superior Court at their regular terms have jurisdiction" and good cause having been shown why such court should be held in the County of Iredell, you are hereby nominated, appointed, and commissioned to hold such court of Oyer and Terminer in said county at such early time as you may appoint. In witness whereof His Excellency Jonathan Worth, our governor – Captain General and commander in chief has hereunto set his hand and caused the great seal of the State to be affixed.

Done at the City of Raleigh this thirteenth day of December in the year of our Lord one thousand, eight-hundred and sixty-seven and in the ninety-second year of our Independence.

Jonathan Worth

By the governor
W.H. Bagby, private secretary

And at said term of court of Oyer and Terminer
The following proceedings were had, to wit:

State	Murder
vs	
Thomas Dula &	
Ann Melton	

The prisoners being brought to the bar of the Court Whereupon the following order was made Ordered by the Court that the Sheriff of Iredell County summon a special venue of one hundred jurors to appear on Tuesday morning of the Term at the hour of 10 o'clock.

Prisoners remanded to jail. Court adjourned until Tuesday morning 10 o'clock.

(Tuesday morning, January 21,1868, Tom Dula again filed an affidavit for severance.)

It is ordered by the Court that there be a severance in the case and the prisoners to be tried separately.

State	Murder	Pleas not guilty
vs		
Thomas Dula		

The following jury to wit:

1. Albertus Cornelius
2. A.P. Sharpe
3. Samuel Dockery
4. Wm. Mears
5. James Lipe
6. Eli Bost
7. R.I. Davidson
8. Hiram Hastings
9. R.O. Sendler
10. Archibald Hoover
11. Willis Hooper
12. Dagwall Harkey

Being chosen, tried, and sworn to speak the truth of and concerning the premises upon their oath say that the said Thomas Dula is guilty of the felony and murder in manner and form as charged in the bill of indictment.

Motion in arrest of Judgment; motion overruled and judgment being prayed by the solicitor and upon this it is demanded of the said Thomas Dula if he have anything to say wherefore the court here ought to proceed and verdict aforesaid to proceed to judgment and execution against him, who nothing further saith than he has already said. Whereupon all and singular the prisoner being seen and by the Court here that the said Thomas Dula be taken to the Jail of Iredell County whence he came, there to remain until the 14th day of February, 1868 and that on that day he be taken by the Sheriff of said County to the place of public execution of said county between the hours of 10 o'clock am and 4 o'clock pm, and there hanged by the neck until he be dead: From the said Judgment the said Thomas Dula prayed an appeal the Supreme Court, and it appearing to the satisfaction of the Court here that the said Thomas Dula is insolvent the said Thomas Dula is allowed to appeal without security.

The prisoners remanded to jail.

5. Judge's Summary

The following is the summary of the case made out by the Honorable William M. Shipp, who presided at Tom Dula's second trial:

This was an indictment for murder, tried at a court of Oyer and Terminer for Iredell County. The indictment charged the prisoner Thomas Dula as principal in the murder of one Laura Foster of Wilkes County, and Ann Melton as accessory before the fact. The State relied upon circumstantial testimony to prove the homicide and upon the declarations and acts of Ann Melton in furtherance of an alleged agreement between the prisoner and the said Ann Melton, to commit the homicide. In order to establish the agreement between the parties it was in evidence to the court alone that Laura Foster was at home, at her father's house on Thursday night, the 24th day of May, 1866; that on Friday morning she was gone; that a mare tied in the yard was likewise gone. She (Laura) was seen early Friday morning riding the mare which belonged to her father, about a mile from home, going in the direction of a place known as the Bates place. She was not seen by any witness after that time.

A body was subsequently found near the Bates Place, buried in a rude manner in a remote place in a thicket of Laurel. This body was identified by her father and several other witnesses who swore that they knew it from the clothes and from the teeth, and the hair. The physician who examined the body swore that there was a wound on the left side near the heart, piercing through the dress (which) was found upon her, and into the cavity of her body.

It was in evidence by the father of Laura Foster that the prisoner had visited her frequently before the alleged homicide; that he had been seen in bed with her on one or two occasions. It was in evidence by the father that she had sores upon her person and that she had been taking medicine. It was in evidence by a physician that Thomas Dula had said to him in March, 1866, that he had a venereal disease called syphilis and that he had contracted that disease from Laura Foster. The physician treated him for that disease; he stated that the disease was in its primary stage. It was in evidence by another person that the prisoner told him previous to the alleged homicide that he had this disease and that he intended to put the one through who gave it to him.

It was in evidence that the prisoner was at the house of the deceased on the Saturday previous to her death, that he was there on the Wednesday previous to that time, and that on both occasions he had private conversation with her. It was testified to that he was seen Friday morning, the same day on which the deceased left home, near her father's house, travelling on a road parallel to the one on which the girl was going. This road led among other places to the Bates Place, and was nearer than the one on which the girl was travelling. It was in evidence that the prisoner went to the house of Ann Melton on that Friday morning, found her in bed, and leant over and had a whispered conversation with her. It was in evidence that the prisoner on Thursday was at the house of Ann Melton, that he sent a man for a quart of liquor that on the same day he went to the mother of Ann Melton and borrowed a mattock; he was seen with the same mattock a few hundred yards from where the grave was found on the same evening. It was in evidence that the quart of liquor was brought by the messenger to Ann Melton's house in the absence of the prisoner. It was in evidence by the sister and mother of Ann Melton that she came to their house (where the prisoner had borrowed the mattock) and that she requested a little girl to go down to the prisoner's mother's and tell him to come up and get his liquor, but not to tell him if his sister, Eliza, was there but to tread on his toes or pinch him and tell him mother wanted to see him. The girl went down and did not find him. He afterwards came and he and Ann Melton had a private conversation and each went off in opposite directions. It was in evidence that Ann Melton did not return home on Thursday night but that she came home on Friday morning before day with her dress and shoes wet. She remained in bed the greater part of the day on Friday.

There was evidence that Ann Melton and the prisoner had been on most intimate terms for a number of years and that an adulterous intercourse had been kept up between them and that he visited the house daily. It was also in evidence that Ann Melton had a sore mouth and that she had taken medicine for it previous to the death of Laura Foster. It was further proved that Thomas Dula came to Ann Melton's house on Thursday morning and said that he had met Ann Melton on the ridge not far from the house, shortly before that time and that she told him where to get some alum and a canteen; upon this testimony, it was insisted on the part of the state that there was sufficient evidence of an agreement between the prisoner and Ann Melton to commit the alleged homicide to authorize the declarations, admissions, and acts of hers in furtherance of said agreement, to be given in evidence.

The hypothesis on the part of the state was that the grave was dug on Thursday or Thursday night, that the deceased was killed on Friday or Friday night, that the motive for the perpetration of the murder was the resentment caused by the fact that the prisoner had caught a disgusting venereal disease from the deceased and had communicated it to his paramour, Ann Melton. The State offered to prove declarations, admissions, etc. of Ann Melton. This testimony was objected to by the prisoner, but the Court being of the opinion that the evidence stated above, which was testified to by various witnesses, was true and that it established an agreement overruled an agreement (,) overruled the objection (sic).

The Court instructed the jury that the evidence offered to the Court of the acts, etc. of Ann Melton were admitted by the Court for its information as to whether there was an agreement between her and the prisoner to commit the homicide but that this opinion of the court was to have no weight with them when they came to decide upon the prisoner's guilt or innocence upon all the evidence. Prisoner excepts. Various declarations of Ann Melton previous to the alledged (sic) murder threatening vengeance against Laura Foster were proved. Declarations of hers on Thursday previous to the day on which she (Laura) was killed stating that she (Ann) had contracted a venereal disease from the prisoner and that he had got it from Laura Foster and that she intended to have her revenge or that she intended to kill her or have her killed were proved by a witness.

There was evidence of a secret and private conference between them, prisoner and Ann Melton on Thursday morning on the ridge between Ann Melton's and her mother's. The Canteen in which the liquor had been brought to her house by the messenger on Thursday was found by a witness on Friday morning under a tree where Ann Melton told her it was. There was a very small quantity of liquor left in the canteen. It was in evidence to the Jury that the prisoner said he had received the canteen of liquor by a witness who saw him that evening (afternoon) on his way up the River.

There was mass of circumstantial testimony in evidence before the jury tending to show the prisoner's connection with the alleged homicide. All the evidence was submitted to the jury under a charge from the court to which no exception was taken. Among other witnesses, Mrs. Scott was examined who swore that she saw Laura Foster on Friday morning riding on her father's mare with a bundle of clothes travelling in the direction of the place called Bates place, that Laura as she was passing told witnesses that she was going to the Bates place. It was objected to by the prisoner, that the witness should state the declarations of Laura Foster. The Court overruled the objection. The prisoner excepted.

Afterwards in the progress of the argument the solicitor on the part of the State stated that inasmuch as this testimony was objected to on the part of the prisoner, he withdrew it and asked the Court and Jury so to consider it. The prisoner's counsel, in reply to the argument of the solicitor, complained of the course on the part of the prosecution inasmuch as the evidence had been heard by the Jury. The Court in summing up the evidence did not notice the declarations of Laura Foster and treated them as withdrawn. Another witness was examined on the part of the State, a white woman by the name of Eliza Anderson. In the course of the cross-examination, the prisoner's counsel proposed to ask witness if she was related to John Anderson - John Anderson was a man of color. The object as stated was to disparage or discredit her. Upon objection, the question was ruled out. Prisoner excepted. The Jury found the defendant guilty. Motion for a new trial. Motion refused. Motion in arrest of Judgment. Motion overruled. Judgment being pronounced, defendant prayed an appeal to the Supreme Court, which was granted.

W.M. Shipp JSCSE

6. The Unidentified Transcript

The following transcript was among some miscellaneous Wilkes County criminal papers in the State Archives. It contains notes taken during Pauline Foster's testimony, but the time and the place are not indicated. The transcript starts abruptly and breaks off in the middle of a sentence. The original notes are jotted down in fragments with few or no punctuation marks other than dashes. I have tried to make statements of the fragments, generally, and have occasionally added a word or words in brackets to complete the sense of a statement.

Ann Pauline Foster – lived and worked at Mr. Melton – went there last March this year – related to Ann Melton – came from Watauga – age 21 – came to see her grandfather & saw Ann Melton and James. They offered her 21 dollars to work thru this summer – never saw Dula until she came to Dula's (Melton's?) house there the day she went. He was there every day or every night. Came when Melton was away if possible. If not came when he was there. Would stay all night and sleep with Ann – 3 beds in the house. Pauline in one, Ann another & Dula pretend to sleep with M in another. Quarrel between Dula and Thomas Foster. Ann and Tom sometimes fell out. Melton never slept with wife. Dula never slept with Ann frequently while Melton was there. Dula never slept with witness nor Melton. Dula would romp with witness, would say he did it to make people to think (so people would not think) he came to see Ann - would always devote himself to Ann when by themselves. Ann had great influence over Dula. She and Dula were going over to beat Mr. Griffin. Never heard her speak to him about Laura Foster – had heard her quarrel with him about Caroline Barnes. Ann told her (Pauline) she was diseased a short time before (a few days) she threatened Laura. She was very angry. On Thursday morning she told her Dula had given her the disease and that Laura gave it to him. She would fool Melton (who had it) but would have her revenge. She would have to do with Melton and make him think he gave it to her. She said she was going to kill Laura Foster and if I (witness) should leave that place that day or talk about (it) with anybody she would kill me – did not call Dula's name said she would (go) to her mothers – and take the liquor to Dula – (Carson Dula returned about 10 o'clock with liquor) – when she (Pauline) returned from the field the liquor was there. Ann took the canteen and left with it. Took a drink before she left – said it was for Dula. That morning two hours after Dula and Carson Dula left, Ann came back. Dula and she would have probably met. Ann did not come back until about an hour before day next morning. Shoes and tail of her dress were wet. She pulled off (shoes and dress) and got in bed. Said her and her mother and Dula had laid out that night and drunk that canteen of liquor. Melton was afraid to ask her any questions about anything. Ann boasted that she could make Dula do anything, that she always kept everybody under her control. Ann was scarcely up when witness came back from field. Wilson Foster came at night, then Tom (Foster), then Washington Anderson, then Will Holder. Gilbert was there working. Witness said to Tom Foster, "When have you seen Dula?" He said, "He saw him that evening." Wilson Foster said he reckoned they (Laura and Tom) had got married and gone off with his mare. Ann got up late before bedtime and put on her clothes. Tom Foster and witness sat up and talked until past midnight. Didn't miss Ann at all. Saturday morning she said "she'd done what she said." Said she got up in the night and Pauline and Tom (Foster) knew nothing about it. On Saturday or Sunday she said she had killed Laura Foster. (She) commenced cussing about that disease. After seeing Dula Thursday morning I didn't see him any more until Friday morning. Was starting out to work. Came back to get her milk vessels. Dula and Ann were talking secretly when she entered the house. Ann was lying on the bed. Didn't see Dula (after that) until Saturday morning tolerably early. Wanted James to fix shoes or fiddle. Dula and Ann talked a long time. Witness told she thought he and Laura Foster had run off. Dula laughed and said "What use do you suppose I would have for Laura Foster?" That night Dula returned and brought his fiddle, played it until bedtime. Played witness to sleep. Came every day or night until he went to Tennessee. Frequently mentioned report to Dula that he had killed Laura Foster. He would laugh and say they would have to prove it and he would whip them besides. The night he ran away he came (four weeks after the murder). Ann pulled a board off inside the wall, punched the dirt out, put her knife under her pillow, drew a nail outside, put a string around her wrist for Dula to pull. Said she would fight for Dula if they arrested him. James Melton learned Dula was about to be arrested and told him in witness's presence. Dula cussed the Hendrickses about it. About 1:20 o'clock, Dula went off after a while. This was Sunday. Ann said he came back next morning and then went up to Hendricks'. He came back about dark (Ann had fixed the knife, string, etc.) from towards the Hendricks's. Hadn't much to say. Appeared as if his feelings were hurt. Said he was going home that night. Said wouldn't stay, but changed his mind and lay down on bed. Dula then cried. Ann went out in the yard. Witness and Dula went out in the yard to Ann. Dula denied it (the murder). Said he was going to leave. Would come back Christmas for his mother and would take Ann with him. Had his arms around Ann. Both crying. Dula told them both good-by. Heard him crying. Ann cried so that Melton asked her what was the matter. She said "Dula was leaving." Dula had a Bowie knife. Carried it in a pocket made in his coat. Description of knife. About three weeks afterwards witness went to Watauga with her brother. Taylor Land heard conversation with Ann about it (leaving). Ann was not milking. Followed Pauline some distance to get her back. Dula had been brought back and put in jail before she left. Ann Melton and Sam Foster came to Watauga after witness. She (Pauline) came (back) with her. Ann told Pauline that they were talking about arresting her (Pauline) and induced her to come back. Ann frequently sent things to Dula. About 3 weeks after Pauline came back from Watauga, Ann, crying, said, "Poor Dula. I wonder if he will be hung. Are you a friend of Dula? I am. Are you a friend of mine. I want to show you Laura Foster's grave. They have pretty well quit hunting for it. I want to see whether it looks suspicious." If so she would carry body to cabbage patch soon next morning and work over. Then changed her notion and said "no that won't do. I will take her over and put her in the big (several words are obscure here). Would cut her up and put her in a bag and carry her. They started to the grave. Went up ridge road to Lotty Fosters, then off through an old field, then crossed Reedy Branch, then mounted another ridge and came to a pine log, where the dirt was apparently rooted up by hogs. Ann said the grave was up further between trees (and) ivy bushes. Covered up the ground with leaves to prevent suspicion. Pauline refused to go further. Ann wanted to go to the grave, and cussed witness terribly until they got to the creek (branch). Told witness at the creek that if she ever told this, she (Ann) would put witness where Laura Foster was. When they got near home, (Ann) pretended it was a dream. About a week afterwards, John (Jack) Adkins and Ben Ferguson came to Melton's. All sitting there talking. Ben said he believed witness helped kill Laura Foster and ran to Watauga on account of it. Witness said, "Yes, Tom and I did kill Laura," squeezing Adkin's hand and laughing at him. Ann said, "You have said enough to hang you and Dula both, but you said it in a joke." Then joke with a rope, etc. (The transcript ends abruptly here.)

7. Final Legal Entry

State of N.C.
Iredell County

Be it remembered that a Superior Court of Law was opened held for the county of Iredell at the court house in Statesville on the 7th Monday after the last Monday in February AD 1868 it being the 13 day of April in said year. The Honorable Anderson Mitchell one of the judges in and for said state present and presiding.

The following to wit appears:

State	Murder
vs.	
Thomas Dula	

It is ordered by the Court that the prisoner Thomas Dula be brought to the bar of the Court by the Sheriff of Iredell County. The prisoner Thomas Dula being brought to the bar of the Court, by the sheriff of Iredell County in whose custody he is. It being by the solicitor for the State that the Court pass judgment upon the prisoner and upon that it is demanded of the said Thomas Dula, if he hath anything to say wherefore the Court here ought not upon the premises and verdict aforesaid to proceed to judgment and Execution against him. Whereupon all and singular the premises being seen and by the Court here being fully understood it is considered by the Court here that the said Thomas Dula be taken to the Jail of Iredell County whence (he) came, there to remain until Friday, the 1st of May AD 1868, and that on that date he be taken by the Sheriff of said county to the place of public Execution of said county between the hours of 12 o'clock (noon) and four P.M. and there be hanged by the neck until he be dead. It appearing to the satisfaction of the Court here that the prisoner Thomas Dula is unable to pay the cost of this prosecution It is therefore considered and adjudged by the Court here that the County of Wilkes pay the costs of this prosecution.

State	Bill costs in Wilkes County
vs.	
Thomas Dula	to wit

2 indictments & certificates			2.40
4 orders			1.20
2 Capias's(es)			2.25
11 Subpoenas		2.37 1/2	23.37 1/2
7 Seals			2.00
17 Probates			2.53
21 Recogniances (recognizances)			6.30
1 Affidavit .			.30
Transcript seal			3.37
George N. Carter	State witness		15.30
C.C. Jones	" "		7.80
J.M. Isbell	" "		7.80
Calvin Carlton	" "		8.00
Wilson Foster	" "		8.40
James Melton	" "		12.04
Thomas Foster	" "		4.80
H. Kendall	" "		4.74
Ben Ferguson	" "		4.38
Carson Dula	" "		4.80
Bennett Walsh	" "		12.30
G.W. Anderson	" "		1.92
Wilson Foster	" "		5.10
James Foster	" "		5.10
Tempy Pilkerton	" "		3.30
J.C.Horton	" "		7.10
J.W. Winkler	Def. Wit.		5.10
			118.18
W.H. Witherspoon	D.S.		2.70
P. Tomlinson	D.S.		1.50
W. White	D.S.		8.00
Thomas McNeil	Guard		2.10
B.F. McNeil	"		2.16
Poindexter Jones			1.96
Lee Saintclair	Guard		2.16
E. Cranor	Jailor		100.95
			103.11

Costs in Iredell Superior Court

Entering	C. L. S. Clk	.60
3 Continuances	C. L. S. Clk	.90
49 Subpoenas	State " "	7.35
45 Seals	State " "	11.25
Postage on same	" "	.36
2 Motions in arrest of Judgement		.60
2 " for new Trial	"	.60
3 Orders	"	.90
2 Appeals	"	1.20
35 Recognizances	"	7.00
3 Transcripts & Postage Superior Court Clk.		8.57
Judgement and bill	"	1.10
1 Affidavit	"	.20
G.W. Brown Clk 4 Subpoenas		.60
2 Seals		.50
		41.73

Sheriff Wm. F. Wasson summoning	
3 special Venue 100 each	60.00
Executing subpoenas	1.50
Sheriff Wasson 2 Juries counted (?)	.20
" " Executing prisoner	10.00
	71.70

D. S. W. T. Watts Executing and Subp.	.30
Sheriff John Horton	.30
Sheriff R.R. Call	6.30
D. S. Ed Brown	1.20
" J.A. Wakefield	.30
" J.L. Laxton	1.80
" R.D. Hall	.60
Sheriff W.G. Hix	.60
" " " " Conveying prisoner to Iredell	8.00
" 1 guard	4.00
D. S. W. H. Witherspoon	24.30
	47.70

State Witnesses	
Franklin West (to use Miller and Vanfelt)	14.50

R.D. Hall	(to use Templeton & McLean)	8.30
J.G. Melton	" "	7.80
Jos Howard col	" "	8.10
A.P. Scott	" "	13.40
C. Dula	" "	8.10
Thos. M. Dula	" "	7.70
W.C. Dula	" "	8.10
J.G. Jones	" "	8.10
Dr. G.N. Carter	" "	13.70
L.B. Welch	" "	8.20
		91.70
Ben Ferguson (to use Templeton & McLean)		7.60
James Scott	" "	9.45
R.D. Hall	" "	8.05
W.G. Melton	" "	9.55
B.H. Welch	" "	9.55
M.C. Hendricks	" "	10.50
Carson Dula	" "	9.55
Calvin Carlton	" "	9.65
Elizabeth Scott	" "	9.65
B.D. Ferguson	" "	9.65
John Adkins	" "	9.15
J.M. Isbell	" "	9.15
R.D. Horton	" "	9.15
G.N. Carter	" "	9.15
Wilson Foster	" "	9.65
Hezekiah Kendall	" "	9.65
J.W. Winkler	" "	5.70
Eliza Anderson	" "	9.45
Martha Gilbert	" "	9.25
J.P. Hoffman	" "	9.90
Pauline Foster	" "	14.65
Lotty Foster	" "	9.25
Samuel Foster	" "	9.25
Tempe Pilkerton	" "	9.25
Thomas Foster	" "	9.25
Celia Scott	" "	9.45
G.W. Anderson	" "	9.45
		244.55

C.P. Jones	27.70
G.N. Carter	13.60
D.E. Horton	21.30
Angeline Scott	6.60
G.H. Brown	7.15
	76.35

W.H. Witherspoon	20.20
Martha Foster (to use W.H. Witherspoon)	13.20
Richard Swanson " "	14.10
Lucinda Witherspoon " "	14.40
Theodocia " "	13.40
	76.00
Phenias Horton	13.40
G.W. Hendricks (to use Phenias Horton)	11.60
Lydney Welch " "	14.30
John Hoffman " "	21.15
J.M. Isbell " "	27.30
D.P. Adkins " "	30.70
Thomas Hall " "	14.10
Wm. Adkins " "	14.30
George Triplett " "	22.20
Gay Hendricks " "	30.30
Leeander Hendricks " "	20.95
Elizabeth Scott " "	30.75
R.D. Hall " "	20.50
Cynthia Dula " "	14.10
Micajah Hendricks " "	31.25
Samuel Foster " "	19.50
Lotty Foster " "	20.20
Tiny Foster " "	20.20
Thomas M. Dula " "	19.70
B.D. Ferguson " "	13.60
Wilson Foster " "	29.30
James Foster " "	29.30
Alfred Witherspoon Col " "	13.60
Jesse Gilbert " "	14.10

Drewry Adkins	"	"	4.53
J.H. Jones	"	"	21.10
Celia Scott	"	"	20.90
B.H. Welch	"	"	30.90
C. Carlton	"	"	28.80
W. German	"	"	27.30
Beckia Gilbert	"	"	14.10
Rufus D. Horton	"	"	13.40
Rebecca Anderson	"	"	13.70
James Anderson	"	"	13.70
Eliza Anderson	"	"	19.90
G.W. Anderson	"	"	20.80
T.E. Witherspoon	"	"	5.60
H. Kendall	"	"	6.40
Alexander Melton	"	"	6.80
J.H. Adkins	"	"	9.10
J.G. Melton	"	"	6.60
Martha Foster	"	"	6.20
C. Dula	"	"	6.50
Martha Gilbert	"	"	6.40
Jos. Howard Col	"	"	14.20
James C. Horton	"	"	13.10
			806.42

C.L. Summers this Transcript	
24 copy sheets	$2.40
1 seal	2.65
	$1,924.10
J.W. Winkler Debts credit	5.30
	$1,913.80

State of North Carolina
Iredell County   C.L. Summers
Clerk Superior court for the County of Iredell do testify that the fore-
going contains a full and perfect transcript of State cost in the case the
State against Thomas Dula. In testimony whereof I hereunto subscribe
my name and affix the seal of said court in Statesville this 19th day of
June 1868.

C.L. Summers Clk.

8. Rulings of the State Supreme Court

State v. Thomas Dula (First ruling by N.C. Supreme Court)

1. To the rule requiring testimony to be subjected to the tests of "an oath" and "cross examination" there are exceptions, arising from necessity. One of these consists of declarations, which are part of the res gestae.
2. This exception embraces only such declarations as give character to an act; therefore, when the deceased was met a few miles from the place where she was murdered, going in the direction of that place, Held that her declarations, in a conversation with the witness, as to where the prisoner was and that she expected to meet him at the place whither she was going, were not admissible against him.
3. That the facts amount to an agreement to commit a crime between the prisoner and one charged as accessory, so as to render competent the acts and declarations of the alleged accessory, is a question of law, and the decision of the court below upon it is subject to review in the Supreme Court.
4. So, whether there is any evidence of a common design. But whether the evidence proves the fact of common design, whether the witnesses are worthy of credit, and in case of conflict, what witnesses should be believed by the Judge, are questions of fact for him to decide, and are not liable to review.

(State v. George, 29 N.C., 321, and State v. Andrew, ante, p. 205, cited and approved.)

Murder, tried before Buxton, J., at Fall Term, 1866, of the Superior Court of Iredell.

The prisoner was indicted as principal, and one Ann Melton as accessory before the fact, in the murder of one Laura Foster, in Wilkes County in May, 1866. The bill was found at Fall Term, 1866, of Wilkes County Superior Court, and upon affidavit, removed to Iredell. The prisoner and Ann Melton were arraigned together, but, upon motion of the counsel for the former, there was a severance, and he put upon his trial alone.

The case, as made out by his Honor, contained a statement of all the evidence, and was quite voluminous. There were several exceptions by the prisoner on account of the admission of improper testimony. The opinion of this court makes it unnecessary to state them all, or to detail the evidence.

The body of the deceased was found a few weeks after she disappeared near a locality called "the Bates place," and was recognized. There were plain indications that the deceased had been murdered; and the testimony relied on to prove the guilt of the prisoner was circumstantial.

One Betsy Scott testified that she saw the deceased the morning of the day she was missing; "she was riding her father's mare, bareback, with a bundle of clothes in her lap," etc. It was then proposed to prove by the witness that in a conversation that ensued between her and the deceased, the latter said she was on her way to the Bates place; that the prisoner had returned just before day, was going another way, and she expected to meet him at the Bates place. The prisoner objected to the declarations, as not being a part of the res gestae; but the testimony was admitted.

The other exceptions were principally to the admission of evidence of acts and declarations of Ann Melton. The prisoner contended that such evidence should not go to the jury, unless a common design between him and Ann Melton had first been established. His Honor overruled the exceptions, and the testimony was admitted.

Verdict of Guilty; Rule for a new trial; Rule discharged; Motion in arrest of judgment; Motion overruled; Judgment of Death, and Appeal.

Attorney General and Boyden, for the State.
Vance, for the prisoner.

Pearson, C.J. The case discloses a most horrible murder, and the public interest demands that the perpetrator of the crime should suffer death; but the public interest also demands that the prisoner, even if he be guilty, shall not be convicted, unless his guilt can be proved according to the law of the land.

The conversation between Mrs. Scott and the deceased ought not to have been admitted as evidence. At all events, no part of it except that the deceased was going to the Bates place. How what the deceased said in regard to the prisoner's having come just before day, and where he was, and that she expected to meet him, can in any case be considered a part of the acts of the deceased - being on her father's mare, bare back, with a bundle of clothes in her lap, and coming from her father's past A. Scott's house, when the witness met her in the road - we are unable to perceive. The law requires all testimony, which is given to the jury, to be subjected to two tests of its truth: 1st. It must have the sanction of an oath. 2nd. There must be an opportunity of cross-examination. Dying declarations form an exception, and another exception is allowed when declarations constitute a part of the act, or res gestae. Acts frequently constitute not only of an action or thing being done, but of words showing the nature and quality of the thing. In such cases, when the action or thing being done is offered in evidence, as a matter of course the words which form a part of it must also be received in evidence; as if one seizes another by the arm, saying, I arrest you under a State's warrant, these words are just as much a part of the act done as the action of taking him by the arm.

In the case of this conversation between Mrs. Scott and the deceased, although it occurred at the time of the action or thing being done, to wit, her being in the road on her father's mare, bare back, cannot, in any point of view, be considered a part of the act. It was entirely accidental, and consisted simply of answers to inquiries which the curiosity of Mrs. Scott induced her to make. These answers may have been true, or they may have been false, but they were not verified by "the tests" which the law of evidence requires, and it was error to admit them as evidence against the prisoner.

As the case must go back for another trial, we do not feel at liberty to enter into an expression of opinion in regard to the other matters of exception. But we see from the case sent that His Honor fell into the error, for which a venire de nova is awarded at this term in State v. Andrew. That is, without stating distinctly how he decided the facts, preliminary to the admission of the acts and declarations of Ann Melton in furtherance of a common purpose to murder the deceased, upon the evidence offered to the courts to establish these preliminary acts he allows the evidence to the jury, and instructs them that if they are not satisfied of the existence of a conspiracy between the prisoner and Ann Melton to effect the murder of the deceased, in that case they are to give to the acts and declarations of Ann Melton, which had been admitted as evidence to them no weight, and are not to be influenced by them. What facts amount to such an agreement between the prisoner and Ann Melton, to give aid and assist each other in effecting the murder of the deceased, as to make her acts and declarations in furtherance of the common purpose evidence against him, is a question of law, and the decision in the court below may be reviewed in this court; so, what evidence the Judge should allow to be offered to him to establish these facts, is a question of law; so, whether there is any evidence tending to show the existence of such an agreement is a question of law. But whether the evidence, if true, proves these facts, and whether the witness giving testimony to the court touching the facts are entitled to credit or not, and, in the case of a conflict of testimony, which witness should be believed by the court, are questions of fact to be decided by the Judge, and his decision cannot be reviewed in this court. See State v. George, 29 N.C., 321, and State v. Andrew, decided at this term, ante, p. 205, where the subject is fully explained. The remarks made in that case are applicable to this, not excepting what is said in reference to the prolixity of cases made up for this court.

In speaking of the connection necessary to be found between the prisoner and Ann Melton as preliminary to this admissibility of her acts and declarations, in furtherance of the common purpose, in evidence against him, I have used the word "agreement" to aid and assist each other to effect the death, in preference to the word conspiracy; for, although they have the same meaning, yet the latter is apt to lead to a confusion of ideas. If parties are indicted for a conspiracy to murder or do some other unlawful act, in that case the issue joined on the plea of not guilty is the fact of the conspiracy; the endeavor to prove it must, of course, be given to the jury and passed upon by them. Otherwise, where the indictment is for the murder or other act, and the fact of an agreement is to aid and assist is only preliminary to the admissibility of the acts and declarations of one against the other.

Per Curiam.   *Venire de novo*
Cited: State v. Dula, post 440, Devries v. Phillips, 63 N.C., 208.

9. The State vs. Tom Dula

(Ruling on second trial by N.C. Supreme Court)

1. Where there is any evidence of an agreement between two or more to compass the death of a third person, the decision of the court below that such evidence is sufficient to establish the agreement, (preliminary to the admission of the acts, etc., of one of such persons as evidence against the other), cannot be reviewed in the Supreme Court.
2. Although in investigating the preliminary question as to the agreement, evidence of the naked declarations of one of the parties is not competent; yet if such declarations make part of the act charged in the indictment, it is otherwise.
3. In order to support an exception to the exclusion of certain testimony, such testimony must appear to have been relevant.
4. What one says in via, as to the place to which he is going, is competent evidence to establish the truth of what he says.
5. It is no ground for an arrest of judgment that the name of the State is omitted in the body of the indictment; or that the memorandum of the pleas of two defendants is prefaced by the word "saith."

(State v. Dula, ante 211, and State v. Lane, 26 N.C., 113, cited and approved.)

Murder, tried at a court of Oyer and Terminer for Iredell, upon the third Monday of January 1868, before Shipp, J.

The prisoner was charged as principal in the murder of one Laura Foster, in Wilkes County, in January 1866; one Ann Melton being charged in the same indictment as accessory before the fact, but not being upon trial, in consequence of an affidavit made by the prisoner.

The State relied upon circumstantial testimony, and upon the acts and declarations of Ann Melton in furtherance of an alleged agreement between her and the prisoner to commit the homicide. To establish the agreement evidence was given to the court that the deceased was at home, at her father's on Thursday night the 24th of January, but on the next morning was gone, as was also a mare that had been tied in the yard. Early on Friday she was seen upon the mare, about a mile from home, going in the direction of "the Bates place." She was not seen alive after that, but subsequently her body was found rudely buried in a laurel thicket near that place, and there was a wound upon her left side piercing the cavity of the body. There was evidence that the prisoner was in the habit of criminal intercourse with both the deceased and Ann Melton; that some short while before he had contracted a disease from the deceased and had communicated it to Ann Melton; that he had threatened to "put through" whoever had given it to him; that he had been with the deceased at her home on the Sunday and Monday before she disappeared and there had private conversations with her; that on Thursday and Friday he had had private interviews with Ann Melton at her home, and on a ridge near her home; that he had sent for liquor in a canteen when at her home on Thursday, which was brought there in his absence; whereupon Ann Melton had sent for him by a little girl, in a secret and singular manner, to come and get it, but her messenger did not find him; that afterwards he had come to her mother's house, and after a private conversation between them, he and Ann went off in opposite directions; that during the same day he had been at Ann Melton's house, saying, he had met her upon a ridge near by, and that she had told him where to get the canteen and some alum; that he had borrowed a mattock during the day from her mother and was seen with it near "the Bates place"; that on Friday morning he was seen traveling in the direction of "the Bates place," by a road which parallel to that by which Laura Foster was seen going; that Ann Melton, after leaving her mother's, did not return to her own house until Friday morning, when her shoes and dress were wet, and she retired to bed, remaining there most of the day; after she had gone to bed the prisoner came there, leaned over her, and had a whispered conversation with her.

The hypothesis of the State was that the grave was dug on Thursday or Thursday night, and the deceased killed on Friday or Friday night; and that the motive was the communication of the disease.

On motion of the State, the court held that the above circumstances were sufficient to authorize the introduction of Ann Melton's acts and declarations in furtherance of the common design; cautioning the jury at the same time that this decision was to have no weight with them as to the prisoner's guilt or innocence.

To this decision the prisoner excepted; as he did specially to the Court's hearing evidence, whilst taking information upon that point, as to the message sent by the little girl.

Evidence was admitted that Laura Foster had said to a witness, whilst riding in the direction of the Bates place, that she was going to that place. To this the prisoner had excepted, and at a subsequent stage of the trial the State agreed that it should not be considered as in evidence and the court thereupon, in charging the jury, told them not to regard it. The prisoner complained of the admission as calculated to prejudice him before the jury.

One Eliza Anderson (a white woman), a witness for the State, was asked upon cross examination, if she was related to John Anderson (a man of color), and the object of this question was stated to be, her disparagement or discredit. Upon objection, the question was ruled out.

Verdict, Guilty; Rule for a New Trial discharged. Judgment, and Appeal.

Vance for the prisoner.
Attorney General, Boyden and Clement, contra.

Pearson, C.J. The case, as it now comes up, presents but few points, and no one of them calls for much discussion.

1st. On the argument, the point made upon the evidence offered to the court as preliminary to the admissibility of the acts and declarations of Ann Melton in evidence to the jury against the prisoner, was treated as if the question before this court was in regard to the sufficiency of the evidence to establish the fact of an agreement between Ann Melton and the prisoner to compass the death of Laura Foster; whereas, this court is confined to the question - was there any evidence tending to establish the fact? If so, his Honor's decision, as to its sufficiency, was upon a question of fact, which we cannot review. Looking at it from this point of view, it must be conceded that the point is against the prisoner.

2nd. "His honor erred in receiving as evidence to himself, the declaration of Ann Melton, to wit: the message and instructions given by her to the little girl sent by her to the prisoner." It does not appear on the record that this evidence was objected to as inadmissible. But, suppose it was objected to, we are of the opinion that it was admissible on the ground that, although naked declarations of one are not admissible against the other, to show an agency or an agreement, yet this was not a naked declaration, like an admission or confession, but was a part of the act and, indeed, the most important part of it.

3rd. "The words used by Laura Foster ought not to have been received as evidence." We think that the evidence was admissible as a part of the act. It was so considered by us when the case was up before. Vide ante, 211.

4th. "The question put to the witness, Eliza Anderson, ought not to have been ruled out." There is not enough set out in the statement of the case to show the relevancy of this question, and we are confined to what appears in the statement of the case, treating it as a bill of exceptions on the part of the prisoner.

Neither of the two grounds, taken in support of the motion to arrest the judgment, are tenable. State v. Lane, 26 N.C., 113, is a conclusive answer to one, and the other is only objectionable as violating a rule of grammar. This does not vitiate a legal proceeding when the sense and meaning is clear. Indeed, as the plea of "not guilty" is several and not joint, it would seem to be most proper to use the verb in the singular number and to set out in the record that each person upon the arraignment saith "he is not guilty," "she is not guilty." instead of putting it in the form of a joint plea; but the authorities support the entry in either way.

There is no error. This opinion will be certified to the end, etc.

Per Curiam.   There is no error.

Cited: State v. McNair, 93 N.C., 630; State v. Arnold, 107 N.C., 864

10. Newspaper Articles Contemporary with the Murder

The following article appeared in the *New York Herald* on May 2, 1868 and was reprinted in the *Salisbury Watchman* and *Old North State* on May 8.

THE DEATH PENALTY
Shocking Revelations of Crime and Depravity in North Carolina – Thos. Dula Hanged for the Murder of Laura Foster.

Statesville, N.C.
May 1, 1868

Today took place one of the most singular executions in the annals of crime and under the most extraordinary circumstances on record. A terrible crime was perpetrated and a trial that has not had its equal even in the Burdell trial followed. The evidence was entirely circumstantial; but at nearly half-past two, P.M., Thomas Dula suffered the death penalty, for the murder of Laura Foster, in the presence of nearly three thousand persons of his own race and color.

On the 28th day of May, 1866, a foul inhuman murder was committed in the western portion of Wilkes County, in this State, the victim being Laura Foster, a beautiful, but frail girl, who was decoyed from her father's house in Caldwell County to a place in Wilkes known as the Bates Place, and here brutally murdered. The body was then removed about half a mile from the scene of the murder, and was placed in a grave already prepared for it. Late in August of the same year the body was found in a state of such decomposition that it was difficult to identify it. There was a deep gash in the left breast just above the heart; the wound had evidently been inflicted with a large knife or dagger, causing death instantaneously. It was also believed that the murdered woman was encente (pregnant).

The disappearance of Laura excited no alarm for several days, as it was supposed she had gone off to get married or to visit some acquaintances in Watauga County; but at length the opinion became general that she had been foully dealt with, and a general search was initiated, without success at the time. The community in the vicinity of this tragedy is divided into two entirely separate and distinct classes. The one occupying the fertile lands adjacent to the Yadkin river and its tributaries, is educated and intelligent, and the other, living on the spurs and ridges of the mountains, is ignorant, poor, and depraved. A state of immorality unexampled in the history of any country exists among these people, and such a general system of freeloveism prevails that it is "a wise child that knows its father."

This is the Bates place, where the body was discovered by blood marks, and where some ten or twelve families are living in the manner described. It is a poor country, covered with thickets and a dense undergrowth, and an attempt had been made to conceal the body by covering it with bushes.

Soon suspicion attached to Thos. Dula, a returned Confederate soldier, and one Pauline Foster, an illegitimate cousin of the deceased, and like her also frail, as the guilty parties. Pauline was then servant to Mrs. Melton, and between her and Dula a criminal intimacy was known to exist, and hence suspicion more particularly attached to the culprit, because Pauline had mysteriously disappeared for a time after the murder. Her character was the most abandoned of all, and under the influence of brandy she admitted when asked, that "Tom Dula and me killed Laura;" but apparently recollecting herself, would make no further revelations.

A day subsequent to this, Pauline when (in)criminated by Mrs. Melton, confirmed the above statement, and she was arrested and confined in the jail of Wilkes county. Here she made a confession recriminating Mrs. Melton, who, she alleged, was jealous of Laura, and guided a party to the place where the body was discovered.

Meanwhile, Dula had fled the country, but was pursued and arrested in Tennessee, where he was found under an assumed name. He was then lodged in jail upon the evidence of Pauline, as was also Mrs. Melton, an accessory before the fact. True bills were found against both by the Grand Jury of Wilkes, but upon affidavit of the prisoners the trial was removed to Iredell county.

The most intense interest was maintained in the trial, which lasted several days, by the people here and of the surrounding counties. Nearly all the people on the Bates Place were examined, and the most extraordinary revelations of depraved morality were developed. Wilson Foster, the father of the deceased, testified that when he arose on the morning of Laura's disappearance, his horse was also gone; that he traced the animal to the Bates Place; that he knew the track by a peculiarity in one of the hoofs. He never saw his daughter alive again, but he saw and recognized her body; knew that Dula had been in the habit of visiting his daughter, and had seen them in bed together, and that they had two private conversations on the Monday and Wednesday respectively, preceding her disappearance.

Further testimony went to show that Laura and Dula were both seen on the morning of the murder travelling by different routes from the direction of her home, to the Bates Place, with a view, as was supposed, to marry Dula; that Dula had borrowed a mattock, the implement with which the grave was dug, the day previous, and that he had been heard to say that he contracted a disease from the murdered girl for which he would be revenged upon her. It was also proven that Dula had changed his name, and when being brought back from Tennessee attempted to escape.

This comprised the essential testimony, and the witnesses generally appeared impressed with the idea that Dula was guilty, though some of them appeared anxious to affect an acquittal through fear of some of his reckless associates in the mountains. Another fact attempted to be proved was that the disease contracted by Dula from the murdered woman was imparted by him to Mrs. Melton, who forced him to the commission of the crime on that account. An appeal was granted from the first trial, and a second one had, when the same witnesses were examined, the same testimony elicited, and the same state of excitement existed. Gov. Vance and his assistant counsel for the defense, made powerful forensic efforts which were considered models of ability, but such was the evidence that no other verdict than that of guilty could be rendered.

Mrs. Ann Melton has not yet been tried, though she was present at both of Dula's trials, and, like him, heard his sentence without exhibiting any visible emotion. She is apparently about twenty-five years of age, is the illegitimate daughter of one Carlotta (Lotty) Foster, and is a most beautiful woman. She is entirely uneducated, and though living in the midst of depravity and ignorance has the manner and bearing of an accomplished lady, and all the natural powers that should grace a high born beauty. This may in part account for the great influence she obtained over Dula, with whom she is illegitimately connected, and also for the fact that he persistently denies all knowledge of her participation in the murder.

Pauline Foster, the principal witness against both the accused, is remarkable for nothing but debasement, and may be dismissed with the statement that she has since married a white man and given birth to a Negro child.

Thomas Dula, the condemned man, is about twenty-five years old, five feet eleven inches high, dark eyes, dark curly hair, and though not handsome might be called good-looking. He fought gallantly in the Confederate service, where he established a reputation for bravery; but since the war closed, has become reckless, demoralized and a desperado, of whom the people in his vicinity had a terror. There is everything in his expression to indicate the hardened assassin - a fierce glare of the eyes, a great deal of malignity, and a callousness that is revolting. He laughs and jokes when spoken to of his approaching end, and exhibits a shocking indifference as to the hereafter, refusing persistently all spiritual comfort from attending clergymen.

Yesterday evening his sister and her husband who came with a wagon to take his body, sent him a note from his aged mother, entreating him to confess the truth for her sake, so that she would be satisfied with his guilt or innocence. But further than asking that they be allowed to see him, which request was refused, he said nothing. He still remained defiant, nor showed any signs of repentance, and seemed to have some hope of escape, though he did not say so. A confession had been looked for that might exonerate or implicate still further, his alleged accessory, Mrs. Melton, but this he refused to give, and left the impression that she is not guilty and shall not be "bowed" upon by him though the contrary is generally believed.

He partook of a hearty supper, laughed and spoke lightly, but ere the jailor left him, it was discovered that his shackles were loose, a link in the chain being filed through with a piece of window glass, which was found concealed in his bed. While this was being adjusted, he glared savagely, and in a jocose manner said it has been so for a month past. Being at last left for the night by the jailor, he requested that Mr. Allison, one of his counsel, be sent for, and while charging him with the strictest injunctions to secrecy while he was living, handed him the following, written in a rude manner with a pencil:

> Statement of Thomas C. Dula – I declare that I am the only person that had any hand in the murder of Laura Foster.
>
> April 30, 1868

Besides this he had written a lengthy statement of his life, but without reference to the murder, which was intended as an exhortation to young men to live virtuously, and not to be led astray in paths of vice as he was. There was nothing remarkable in this document, though it covered fifteen pages.

Left alone in his cell on the last night of his earthly existence, the savage fortitude that had characterized his trials, sentence and imprisonment began to give way, and he nervously paced the floor as far as the chain would reach. This was only interrupted through the whole night by an attempt to court "Nature's sweet restorer," but in vain, if a fitful half hour is excepted, and the condemned, after the weary minutes of that night, saw the last sun he should ever behold shed its glorious light through the bars of the window. After breakfast he sent for his spiritual advisers, and seemed for the first time to make an attempt to pray; but still to them and all others denying his guilt or any knowledge of the murder. The theory seemed to be that he would show the people that he could die "game" with an awful crime resting upon his soul. Early in the morning he was baptized by the Methodist clergyman, and from that time engaged fervently in prayer; but when left alone was heard speaking incoherently, words occasionally dropping from his lips in relation to the murder, but nothing was intelligible. And thus wore away the last hours of the condemned.

So long had the execution been pending, and as the murder was committed in one county, and trial had taken place in another, it became generally known throughout the entire western section of the State. By eleven o'clock, A.M., dense crowds of people thronged the streets, the great number of females being somewhat extraordinary. These, however, came mostly because it was a public day and afforded them an opportunity to make purchases but a certain class indicated by a bronzed complexion, rustic attire, a quid of tobacco in their mouths, and a certain mountaineer look, were evidently attracted by the morbid curiosity to see an execution, so general among the ignorant classes of society. The preliminaries were all arranged by Sheriff Wasson. A gallows constructed of native pine, erected near the railroad depot in an old field - as there is no public place of execution in Statesville - was the place selected for the final tragedy. A guard had been summoned to keep back the crowd and enforce the terrible death penalty, and for the better preservation of order, the bar rooms were closed. The curious numbers of the people who had never seen a gallows before, visited the structure, eyeing it with strange feelings, and as it was merely two up-rights, with a space of about ten feet and a cross piece on top, under which the cart with the condemned has to pass, many singular observations were made.

Previous to his being taken from the jail to the gallows, many of the condemned man's former companions in the army from the mountain region in which he lived appeared upon the streets, and some singular reminiscences of his former life were related. Among them, it was generally believed he murdered the husband of a woman at Wilmington, in this State, during the war, with whom he had criminal intercourse. The opinion of all was that he was a terrible, desperate character, and from their knowledge of his former career an anxiety and singular curiosity was excited among them to see how he died. Few there were who pitied him dying, as they believed him guilty, without a confession, and none sympathized with him.

At eighteen minutes before one o'clock, the guard being formed in hollow square, the condemned was led forth attended by the Sheriff and some assistants, and with a smile upon his features, took his seat in the cart, in which was also his coffin, beside his brother in law. The procession moved slowly through the streets accompanied by large crowds, male and female, whites and blacks, many being in carriages and many on horseback and on foot. While on the way to the gallows he looked cheerful and spoke continually to his sister of the Scriptures, assuring her he had repented and that his peace was made with God. At the gallows throngs of people were already assembled, the number of females being almost equal to that of the males. The few trees in the field were crowded with men and boys, and under every imaginable shade that was present, were huddled together every imaginable species of humanity.

Soon the procession came in sight accompan(i)ed by horse-men dashing over the field dispersing the crowd, and at eight minutes past one the cart was halted under the gallows. The condemned man appeared unaffected by the sight, but talked incessantly to his sister and others of religion, trying to assure them that he has repented. Upon being told by the Sheriff that he could address the assembled crowd, he arose and turning his dark eyes upon them spoke in a loud voice which rang back from the woods as if a demon there was mocking the tone and spirit of a wretch who well knew he was going into eternity with an unconfessed murder upon his mind and falsehood upon his lips. He spoke of his early childhood, his parents, and his subsequent career in the army, referred to the dissolution of the Union, made blasphemous allusions to the Deity, invoking that name to prove assertions that he knew were some of them at least, false. The politics of the country he discussed freely, and upon being informed, in reply to a question of his, that Holden was elected Governor of North Carolina, he branded that person as a secessionist and a man that could not be trusted. His only reference to the murder was a half explanation of the country and the different roads and paths leading to the scene of the murder, in which his only anxiety was to show that some two or three of the witnesses swore falsely against him. He mentioned particularly one, James Isbell, who, he alleged, had perjured himself in the case, and concluded by saying that had there been no lies sworn against him he would not have been there. This concluded his speech, which had lasted nearly one hour, and after apparently affectionate farewell to his sister, who was then removed from the cart, the rope, which all the time had been around his neck, was thrown over the gallows and fastened. Standing there on the brink of eternity, this man, calm in the presence of the vast crowd, refused to admit publicly the murder of which they all believed him to be guilty.

At twenty-four minutes after two, P.M., the cart was moved, and the body of Thomas Dula was suspended between heaven and earth. The fall was about two feet, and the neck was not broken. He breathed about five minutes and did not struggle, the pulse beating ten minutes, and in 13 minutes life was declared extinct by Dr. Campbell, attending surgeon. After hanging for twenty minutes the body was cut down and given to the afflicted relatives of this terrible criminal. Thus closed the career of a man, who, though young in years, ignorant and depraved in character, was one of the most confirmed and hardened criminals of the age in which he lived. As yet the written confession above given has not become known, and the greater anxiety is evinced among the people to ascertain whether he had left any confession that he might be too proud to make them in public. His reticence, however, is accounted for by the wish that he would not implicate his accomplice, Mrs. Ann Melton, now to be tried.

The following article on Tom Dula's first trial appeared in the *Wilmington Daily Dispatch* on October 26, 1866, copied from the *Statesville American:*

The Trial of Thomas Dula for the Murder of Laura Foster

The first trial of Thos. Dula and Ann Melton for the murder of Laura Foster, which took place in Wilkes county some two or three months ago, and removed to Iredell, was commenced before Judge Buxton, last Friday morning. Upon application of Counsel, the case was separated, and Dula put first upon trial. The State's Attorney, W.F. Caldwell, Esq., was aided by Messrs. Clement and N. Boyden, and the prisoner defended by Messrs. R.M. Allison, R.F. Armfield and Gov. Vance. A very large number of witnesses were examined, and the case occupied the whole of Friday, Saturday and the following night; the judge gave his charge to the jury after midnight, and about daybreak the jury brought in a verdict against Thomas - Guilty of Murder. At 8 o'clock Sunday morning, the prisoner was sentenced to be hung on the 9th of November between the hours of 10 and 1 o'clock. An appeal was then taken to the Supreme Court.

All the evidence which led to the conviction was entirely circumstantial, but so connected by a concatenation of circumstances as to leave no reasonable doubt upon the minds of the Jury that the prisoner was at least one of the parties that committed the murder. He was most ably defended by his counsel, as was likewise the prosecution. The patience of Judge Buxton during this long and tedious trial, and his humane and impartial charge to the Jury, in sifting the evidence and giving the prisoner the benefit of every reasonable doubt was but characteristic of an "upright Judge" and profound Jurist, who is an honor to the Bench and the State. During the trial the Court room was thronged with spectators and deep interest manifested in the result. A most foul murder of a young woman had been perpetrated - one who though frail, had been decoyed from her home by her betrayer under promises of marriage, and instead of a bridal chamber, received first a dagger in her heart and plunged uncoffined into a bloody grave. The calendar of crime contains not a darker deed.

The term of the Court having expired, the case of Ann Melton, the supposed confederate and accomplice of Dula, was continued, and, probably will be removed to another county.

The following brief statement of the complicity of parties in the tragedy as adduced by the testimony, may not be uninteresting to the public. Ann Melton is a married woman, young and beautiful, and a paramour of Dula's for several years, and had great influence over him. Laura Foster, a distant relative of Ann's, handsome and young, had likewise succumbed to his amours under promise of marriage, perhaps. Ann Melton and Dula's mother are near neighbors - a half mile apart. Laura Foster resided with her father, five miles distant. It was said that Ann became jealous of Laura and wanted her out of the way, and was perhaps present at the killing, if she did not aid in the deed. Thursday previous to the murder of Laura, which was on Friday, Dula borrowed a mattock of a neighbor, as he said, to work on the road, but no doubt to dig a grave in the woods for Laura. That night, he is supposed to have visited Laura at her father's, and induced her to leave her home under some pretense, before day, she taking her father's horse and travelling one road, while he travelled a parallel road - both leading in the direction of his mother's house, and near Ann Melton's, where Laura's body was afterwards found with a stab in the side. Both Dula and Laura were seen by neighbors as they passed along the two roads, on the morning of the fatal day, and Laura told her acquaintance who questioned her that she was going off to get married, etc. The horse which Laura road afterwards returned to her father's. It was stated that Dula had threatened Laura from cause which had arisen out of their intimacy.

The following article on the second trial of Tom Dula, January 1868, was carried in the *Charlotte Western Democrat*, February 4, 1868, copied from the *Statesville American*:

A Court of Oyer and Terminer, Judge Shipp presiding, was opened for the county of Iredell, at this place, Monday of last week. The case of Thomas Dula, charged with the murder of Laura Foster, was called on Tuesday. More than a hundred witnesses were summoned by the State, most of whom were present, and their examination occupied three days. The Solicitor, Mr. W.P. Caldwell, was aided by Messers. Boyden and Clement, and the accused was defended by Gov. Vance and Messrs. Furches and Allison. The pleadings began Friday afternoon and were concluded the following evening, when the Judge gave his charge to the Jury.

The murder was committed in the county of Wilkes, some eighteen months ago, where the parties resided, and the trial moved to Iredell; and, at the following term of our Superior Court, Dula was convicted and sentenced to be hanged. An appeal was taken to the Supreme Court and a new trial granted.

The Jury retired and in a short while returned with a verdict - "Guilty." Dula was sentenced to be hanged on the second Friday in February. An appeal was then applied for and granted to the Supreme Court now in session; with little hope, however, for a new trial. The prisoner was ably defended by his counsel. The address of Gov. Vance to the Jury was ingenious, eloquent, and distinguished for legal lore of the highest grade; but failed to inspire the minds of the Jury with a "reasonable doubt."

The *Salisbury North State* gives the following statement of the case:

"Thomas Dula, a young man of about twenty-five years of age, is charged with the murder of Miss Laura Foster. And Ann Melton is arraigned as accessory. It appears from the evidence that in May, 1866, Laura Foster arose from her bed in her father's house, about an hour before day, and taking her father's horse, which was tied that night near the door, travelled some miles on a road to a place to which the horse was tracked, and near which her body was subsequently found in the woods. Dula and Mrs. Melton were absent from their homes the night on which Laura Foster left her father's and were seen next morning in the neighborhood of the place where the body of Laura Foster was found buried. It is charged that Mrs. Melton was jealous of the attention paid Laura Foster by Dula, and therefore aided and abetted in the murder. The incidents, as developed before the jury, were of the most thrilling character."

11. A Modern Lawyer's View of the Tom Dula Case

by Ted G. West (Deceased), Attorney at Law, Lenoir, N.C.

I have been familiar with the legend and folklore of the Tom Dula case since early childhood, having heard my parents and other persons living in the general area where the crime was committed discuss it on many occasions. I, of course, have heard many of them express the opinion that Tom Dula was not guilty of the offense for which he was hanged. However, after reaching adulthood and studying and having been engaged in the practice of law for a number of years, I have tended to put little credence in such stories because of an awareness that the gossip concerning most highly publicized or controversial cases have little relation to the actual evidence presented at the trial of the case. In criminal cases as in many other aspects of life, people tend to believe what they want to believe, not what the evidence shows. Therefore, upon being asked to review the material in this volume and to make some comments upon the legal aspects of the case as a lawyer, I approached it with the full expectation of concluding that Tom Dula was given a fair trial with due process of law, found guilty by a jury of his peers beyond a reasonable doubt, and paid the supreme penalty which the law provides. I was somewhat surprised after reviewing this volume to come to the conclusion that at least according to the legal standards of today, Tom Dula's conviction and ultimate execution leaves a great deal of room for doubt.

There are at least four aspects of the Tom Dula case which I think bear interesting comment from the standpoint of a lawyer. I would like to discuss each of the four in order.

Tom Dula was first charged with the crime by warrant dated June 28, 1866, after he had removed himself from Wilkes County to the State of Tennessee. His arrest in Tennessee and removal to Wilkes County was, to say the least, most informal, compared to the legal standards required to extradite a person from another state's jurisdiction under today's procedures. At the time of the issuance of the warrant and at the time that Tom Dula was removed from Tennessee to Wilkes County, Laura Foster's body had not yet been discovered and there was, therefore, only a mere suspicion current in the neighborhood that a crime had actually been committed. As far as the authorities knew,

Laura Foster could have been in Tennessee with Tom Dula or could have been in any other place that she might have decided to go. In spite of this fact, Tom was charged with the crime of murder, removed from Tennessee and placed in jail in Wilkes County.

He stayed in jail from the time of his arrival in Wilkes County until Laura Foster's body was discovered in late August or early September, 1866, a period of approximately two months. During this time there was apparently no effort to give him a hearing, to set a bond, or to afford him any of the other constitutional and procedural safeguards current in today's legal procedures. There can be little doubt that if the same event occurred today in a like manner, and if Tom Dula had not agreed to return to Wilkes County voluntarily, the Governor of Tennessee would certainly not have extradited him against his will until the body was discovered and proof that a crime had been committed had been presented to the authorities.

In addition to this factor, once he was removed to Wilkes County, he would certainly have been entitled to an arraignment within a reasonable period of time and upon the failure of the State to prove at the arraignment that a crime had been committed, he would have been set free until such time as the body of Laura Foster was discovered. I can, therefore, only conclude that his incarceration in the Wilkes County jail for a period of almost sixty days was unlawful and was certainly a violation of his constitutional rights. This fact, however, has little to do with the ultimate issue of his guilt or innocence. It could have been an important aspect of the case only if during the period of the unlawful confinement, Tom Dula had confessed to the crime or if any of the evidence presented at the trial of the case had been obtained as a direct result of his unlawful confinement. In either of these events, the confession and evidence would not have been admitted into the trial. However, since neither of these events occurred, the question of his proper extradition from Tennessee and the question of his unlawful confinement prior to the discovery of the body is only of passing interest, and as stated before, has little to do with the ultimate issue of his guilt or innocence of the crime for which he was executed.

The other two factors in his case which should be commented upon do bear upon the question of his guilt or innocence.

It is an elementary rule of procedural law that statements made by another person not made in the presence of the defendant on trial are not admissible into evidence. This rule has as its basis the reasoning that, first, the statements of the party not in the presence of the defendant cannot be denied by the defendant at the time the statement is made, and second, the statement is not subject to the cross-examination of the defendant or his lawyer. There is one exception to this general rule of evidentiary law which is pertinent to the Tom Dula case - that is, that if prior to the commission of the crime there is a conspiracy or common design to commit an unlawful act between the defendant and the person making the statement, then the statements by the co-conspirator not made in the presence of the defendant may be admitted into evidence at the defendant's trial. This is based on the premise that the pre-existence of the conspiracy makes the statement of one the statement of the other. As the records show, at the trial of Tom Dula, certain statements of Ann Melton made after the date of the death of Laura Foster were admitted into evidence against Tom Dula based upon a finding of the trial judge that there had been a common design or conspiracy to murder between Tom Dula and Ann Melton. A review of the evidence presented in this volume shows clearly, I think, that this ruling by the trial judge was erroneous.

Ann Melton and Tom Dula, the evidence shows, had been engaged in an illicit romance for some years prior to the death of Laura Foster. Tom Dula visited Ann Melton regularly, almost nightly, and in fact slept in the same bed with her with Ann Melton's husband present in the same room. His association with her was obvious and common knowledge throughout the community. The only evidence of any conspiracy between her and Tom Dula to commit murder was certain testimony by witnesses that some time prior to the disappearance of Laura Foster, Ann Melton and Tom Dula had been seen together, had carried on whispered conversations and had generally acted in a somewhat suspicious manner.

In view of their prior relationship, these meetings, conferences and consultations are certainly subject to some interpretation other than that they were conspiring to commit a crime since there was not the slightest evidence of any direct conversation between the two concerning the commission of the crime. One can only conclude therefore, in retrospect, that for the trial judge to hold as a matter of law that there was a conspiracy between Ann Melton and Tom Dula pre-existing the disappearance of Laura Foster to murder her is certainly a loose and prejudicial interpretation of their acts and conduct at that time. If this is true, then any of the statements made by Ann Melton not in the presence of

Tom Dula which were admitted at the trial of the case against Tom Dula should have been excluded.

The fourth and most important aspect of the review of the record which should be commented upon has to do with the evidence proper admitted against the defendant upon which the jury based its verdict. In order to view this in its proper light, it is necessary to give a short resume of the substantive evidence upon which the jury based its finding.

An analysis of the testimony of all the witnesses put on the witness stand by the State shows the following: That Tom Dula had syphilis and on one occasion stated he was going to do harm to the person who gave it to him and on another occasion stated that Laura Foster was the person who gave him the disease. That on the day before Laura Foster's disappearance, Tom Dula was seen with a mattock in his hand near the spot where her grave was discovered some three months later. That the night before Laura's disappearance both Tom Dula and Ann Melton were absent from their homes, and that early on the morning of her disappearance, Laura Foster was seen riding her father's horse with a bundle of clothing in the direction of Bates' Place and that on the same morning Tom Dula was seen going in the same direction. It was further put into evidence that the horse which Laura Foster was riding came home with a part of her halter missing and the missing part of the halter was later discovered near where she and Tom Dula had been seen. That afterwards something that looked like blood was seen near that spot and that some time after Laura Foster disappeared, Dula fled the country. It was further testified to that the grave was ultimately discovered because of certain disclosures that had been made by Ann Melton and that the grave was within a fairly short distance of Tom Dula's house and was within 100 or 200 yards of the spot where Tom Dula had been seen with the mattock the day before Laura Foster disappeared.

This is the sum total of the evidence presented to the jury, from which it concluded beyond a reasonable doubt that Tom Dula had killed Laura Foster. It is obvious that all of this evidence is completely circumstantial. It is further obvious that it certainly raises the suspicion that Tom Dula murdered Laura Foster. That the evidence raises such a suspicion is not the purpose of this analysis. Its purpose is to determine whether or not Tom Dula would have been convicted and executed for the crime under the evidence as presented according to today's legal procedures and legal standards of guilt.

It is a settled rule of law in North Carolina that circumstantial evidence alone is sufficient to support a conviction for a crime. This is true, provided, however, that the circumstantial evidence is so strong and positive that: First, the circumstances pointing to guilt of the defendant must exclude every other reasonable hypothesis and point unerringly toward the guilt of the defendant being tried; and second, it convinces a jury of a prisoner's guilt beyond a reasonable doubt.

I do not think it takes a lawyer to conclude, after reviewing this record, that the evidence presented against Tom Dula does not meet at least one of these standards. The evidence obviously convinced the jury beyond a reasonable doubt of his guilt or it would not have found him guilty. The evidence is not, however, subject only to the interpretation of the guilt of Tom Dula and therefore does not exclude every reasonable hypothesis. It shows only a motive and the opportunity which is generally held insufficient to support a conviction.

The most obvious hypothesis that comes to mind is that Ann Melton killed Laura Foster. Whether she actually did or not is of little consequence to the point being made. The point is that she could have, and this alone is sufficient to raise reasonable doubt that Tom Dula did.

Another reasonable hypothesis which comes to mind is that anyone, known or unknown, within the general neighborhood could have perpetrated the crime, including the witnesses themselves who saw Tom Dula in the general area.

Most certainly Tom Dula could have had a valid reason and explanation for his actions and conduct on or about the time that Laura Foster disappeared other than the act of committing murder. He lived in the general area himself, he frequently passed back and forth on the road on which he was seen. There could have been many reasons why he had a mattock in his hands, including the one which is implied by the cross-examination of his lawyer – that is, that he was skelping the road. Even his conduct in leaving the country is subject to the reasonable conclusion that he wanted to get out of a situation where people were accusing him of such a crime, that the suspicions of the neighborhood made him uncomfortable, or even that he knew Ann Melton or some other party had committed the crime and wanted to protect them from whatever knowledge he had.

If the reader desires to compare further the standard of proof required by the present Supreme Court of North Carolina to convict one of crime upon circumstantial evidence alone, he should read the case of

State vs. Holland, 234 NC 354; State vs. Hendrick, 232 NC 447; and State vs. Coffey, 28 NC 119.

After reviewing this record, I can only conclude that if the Tom Dula case arose today and the evidence admitted against him was identical to the evidence presented in the record of this case, there seems little question but that his conviction at this second trial would have been set aside because of insufficient evidence. Since there was apparently no further direct evidence linking him with the commission of the crime, it seems most likely that he would ultimately have gone free. Apparently the folklore I heard as a child had some substance to it.

12. Bibliography

Ashe, Samuel A., Editor. *Biographical History of North Carolina* 8 volumes. Greensboro, 1907.

Brown, Frank C., Editor. *North Carolina Folklore II & IV.* Durham, North Carolina: Duke University Press, 1952.

Dowd, Clement. *Life of Zebulon B. Vance.* Charlotte, North Carolina, 1897.

Greensboro Daily News, February 1, 1959.

Greensboro Daily News, February 8, 1959.

Hayes, Johnson J. *The Land of Wilkes.* North Wilkesboro, North Carolina: Wilkes County Historical Society, 1962.

Hickerson, Thomas Felix. *Happy Valley.* Chapel Hill, North Carolina: (published by author), 1940.

Isbell, Robert L. *The World of My Childhood.* Lenoir, North Carolina: The Lenoir News Topic, 1955.

North Carolina Reports, Volume 61, June Term, 1866 to January Term 1868, annotated.

Warner, Frank. "Frank Proffit." *Sing Out* (October-November, 1963). p. 10

Winston-Salem Journal, November 17, 1958.